SPECTRUM®
Science
Test Practice

Grade 7

Spectrum®
An imprint of Carson-Dellosa Publishing LLC
Greensboro, North Carolina

Spectrum®
An imprint of Carson-Dellosa Publishing LLC
P.O. Box 35665
Greensboro, NC 27425 USA

ISBN 978-0-7696-8067-5

02-244127784

SCIENCE TEST PRACTICE
Table of Contents
Grade 7

Science Test Practice is for everyone who wants to have a working knowledge of the fundamentals of science. Written with the goal of helping students achieve on science tests, it approaches science through the format of the National Science Education Standards.

The National Science Education Standards were developed by the National Academy of Science, an organization of the leading scientists in the United States. Their goal is for all students to achieve scientific literacy. To be scientifically literate means to be able to understand the richness of the world around us; to be able to make decisions based on the skills and processes that science teaches us; and to approach problems and challenges creatively.

This book is divided into four sections, each one based on a National Science Education Content Standard. This book focuses on content standards A-D: Science as Inquiry, Physical Science, Life Science, and Earth and Space Science, with one section devoted to each standard. Standards E-G, which cover science and technology and science in personal and social perspectives, are covered within the four sections. A correlation chart details the coverage of all standards in the book (see pp. 7-8).

How to Use the Book

Students can begin with the Pretest (pp. 9-14). This test covers all the three major strands of science:

- physical science, which includes how objects move and interact;

- life science, which includes animals, plants, and ecosystems;

- earth and space science, which includes rocks and minerals, the oceans, and the solar system.

After the Pretest, you may wish to complete the test prep practice in order, or complete the sections out of sequence. Before completing the practice pages, students should read *Hints and Strategies for Answering Questions* on page 6.

Finally, the Posttest (pp. 86-91) gives students a chance to practice yet again, applying the knowledge gleaned from the rest of the book. A complete answer key appears at the back of the book.

With its real-life questions and standards-based approach, *Science Test Practice* will engage students; give them solid test-taking hints and practice; and provide them an opportunity to build their confidence for other exams.

Multiple Choice

When you encounter a multiple-choice item, read the question carefully until you are sure of its meaning. After reading the question, read all answer choices carefully. Remember that only one answer is absolutely correct; this will be the one that appears to be the truest. Rule out the answer choices that are obviously wrong and choose the answer that holds true for the science scenario, based on what you have studied. Sometimes you will need to refer to a passage or diagram to find the information you need.

Fill-in-the-Blank

When you have to fill in the blanks in a sentence, paragraph, or diagram, read the entire item carefully. Then read it a second time, pausing to think about the missing words or phrases. You can then begin to plug in the words of which you are certain. If you are not sure about a word or phrase, look for clues in other words of the sentence or paragraph. If a word bank is provided, cross out each word as you use it. Remember that the missing words or phrases must agree with the articles and verbs in the sentence.

Short Response

A short response answer usually includes three to four sentences. When you encounter a short response item, read the question carefully. If necessary, return to a passage or diagram to find relevant information. When you are ready to respond, try to think about one topic sentence that can summarize your answer. Write it down, then add two or three sentences that support your topic sentence.

Extended Response

An extended response, or essay, includes three parts: an introduction where you state your main idea or position, a body where you add details that support your topic idea, and a conclusion where you summarize your topic idea. When you have to write an extended response, read the question carefully. Decide whether you have to write a narrative based on a passage or diagram, or argue your point of view on a subject. Then write an introductory paragraph that explains the topic you want to discuss. In the body of the essay, try to be clear and concise, including only information that is necessary and supports the topic.

National Science Education Content Standards Correlation

As a result of activities in grades 5-8, all students should develop an understanding of the concepts below.

Standard	Pages
CONTENT STANDARD A: Science as inquiry	
Abilities necessary to do scientific inquiry	15-25, 27, 28, 37
To learn about the world in a scientific manner, students need to learn how to ask questions, formulate possible answers, devise experiments to test those answers, and base their conclusions on evidence.	
Understanding about scientific inquiry	26-29, 32, 33, 38, 46, 66, 76
Students need to understand that the investigations used to gather information depend on the question being asked; that scientists use mathematics and technology as they work; and that scientists build on the work other scientists have done, by asking questions about that work and that grow out of that work.	
CONTENT STANDARD B: Physical Science	
Properties and changes of properties in matter	32-37
Motion and forces	38-40
Transfer of energy	41-45
CONTENT STANDARD C: Life Science	
Structure and function in living systems	46-51, 67, 68
Reproduction and heredity	52-57
Regulation and behavior	57, 61, 62, 66
Populations and ecosystems	57, 58-62, 67, 68
Diversity and adaptations of organisms	67-69
CONTENT STANDARD D: Earth and Space Science	
Structure of the earth system	63, 71-80
Earth's history	70, 72, 73, 74
Earth in the solar system	81-85

CONTENT STANDARD E: Science and Technology	
Abilities of technological design	30, 31, 65
Understanding about science and technology	30, 31, 65
CONTENT STANDARD F: Science in Personal and Social Perspectives	
Science can seem removed from everyday life, but it actually surrounds us. Personal hygiene activities are based on scientific reasoning. Understanding the risks and benefits in the world makes students more informed citizens.	
Personal health	30, 31, 51
Populations, resources, and environments	51, 55, 61, 62, 64, 66, 67-69
Natural hazards	63, 69
Risks and benefits	31, 63, 69
Science and technology in society	30, 31
CONTENT STANDARD G: History and Nature of Science	
Science as a human endeavor	30, 31, 41, 49, 55, 56, 65, 69
Science is a pursuit of human beings, with many different skills, backgrounds, qualities, and talents. However, scientists all share curiosity about the world, a tendency to ask questions about what is known, an openness to new ideas, insight, and creativity.	
Nature of science	16, 17, 23-25, 27, 30, 60, 69
History of science	16, 27, 30, 31, 70, 72, 76

Name _____ Date _____

Directions: Read the questions. Choose the truest possible answer.

1. **Which of the following has both chemical and physical properties?**
   - (A) energy
   - (B) matter
   - (C) weight
   - (D) space

2. **What happens during a physical change?**
   - (F) The form and appearance of a substance are changed.
   - (G) The amount of a substance is changed.
   - (H) A new substance is created.
   - (J) A chemical change occurs.

3. **What does a chemical equation describe?**
   - (A) a compound
   - (B) a property
   - (C) an atom
   - (D) a reaction

4. **The elements in the same group on the periodic table have similar _____ .**
   - (F) sizes
   - (G) properties
   - (H) atomic numbers
   - (J) numbers of electrons

5. **An electron dot diagram shows**
   - (A) all the electrons of an atom
   - (B) only the paired electrons
   - (C) only the electrons closest to the nucleus
   - (D) only the electrons farthest from the nucleus

6. **What type of bond is formed when two atoms share electrons?**
   - (F) ionic bond
   - (G) covalent bond
   - (H) hydrogen bond
   - (J) polar bond

7. **The universal solvent is _____ .**
   - (A) air
   - (B) salt
   - (C) water
   - (D) oxygen

8. **A substance with a low pH is _____ .**
   - (F) an acid
   - (G) a base
   - (H) a salt
   - (J) neutral

9. **An object will move only when there is _____ force acting on it.**
   - (A) a consistent
   - (B) a balanced
   - (C) an unbalanced
   - (D) a downward

GO ON

10. **What must be known to determine the weight of an object?**

   (F) only the mass of the object

   (G) only the momentum of the object

   (H) both the momentum of the object and the force of friction acting on the object

   (J) both the mass of the object and its acceleration due to gravity

11. **Which of the following is an example of work being done on an object?**

   (A) Terrell picked up a large box in the office.

   (B) Terrell carried a large box from the office to the auditorium.

   (C) Terrell placed the box on the stage, which was level with the height he was carrying the box.

   (D) Terrell tried to push the box into a corner of the stage, but the box would not move.

12. **The rate at which work is done is _____ .**

   (F) energy

   (G) heat

   (H) power

   (J) momentum

13. **Material that does *not* conduct an electrical charge is a(n) _____ .**

   (A) conductor

   (B) insulator

   (C) semiconductor

   (D) contractor

14. **Why is sunlight such a promising future energy source?**

   (F) It is renewable.

   (G) It is not renewable.

   (H) It is less expensive than other energy sources.

   (J) It is requires little or no equipment to use as an energy source.

15. **Water flowing over a waterfall is often used as a means of producing energy. Where does the water in a waterfall have the most gravitational potential energy?**

   (A) at the top of the waterfall

   (B) as it is falling

   (C) at the bottom of the waterfall

   (D) as it flows away from the waterfall

GO ON

Grade 7 Pretest

Directions: Read the text below. Use information from the text to help you answer questions 16–18.

Maria wanted to understand why objects float. She measured the mass and volume of the following objects: a cork, a penny, a pencil, and a paperclip. Then she filled a beaker with 100 mL of water and placed the objects individually into the beaker. She measured the change in the volume of water for each of the objects. She determined that the density, not the weight of an object, was what determined its ability to float. The items with lower density floated regardless of their weight.

16. **Maria's experiment could *best* explain**
    - (F) why fish swim
    - (G) why warm water rises
    - (H) how buoyancy affects objects
    - (J) how gravity affects objects

17. **What would *not* be a factor that changes in this experiment?**
    - (A) mass of the object
    - (B) volume of the object
    - (C) volume of water displaced
    - (D) original volume of the water

18. **What type of variables are mass and volume?**
    - (F) dependent
    - (G) independent
    - (H) controlled
    - (J) special

Directions: Read the questions. Choose the truest possible answer.

19. **What is the innermost layer of Earth?**
    - (A) the core
    - (B) the mantle
    - (C) the crust
    - (D) the lithosphere

20. **Which theory helps to explain how volcanoes and earthquakes occur?**
    - (F) evolution
    - (G) thermodynamics
    - (H) plate tectonics
    - (J) geography

21. **What is the *best* way to describe how soil is formed?**
    - (A) Rivers and oceans flooded the land and left behind sediment, which formed the soil that exists today.
    - (B) Organic material from plants and animals hardens, and over time it forms rock and other material found in bedrock.
    - (C) Lava from under Earth's surface flows out of volcanoes to form all of the soil found on Earth.
    - (D) Over long periods of time, bedrock weathers, plants add organic material to the soil, and rain spreads minerals throughout the layers of soil.

22. **Humus is formed by _____ .**
    - (F) decomposition
    - (G) weathering
    - (H) erosion
    - (J) abrasion

23. **What human activity was the largest contributor to the wind erosion that occurred during the Dust Bowl?**
    - (A) polluting the atmosphere
    - (B) gold mining
    - (C) recycling
    - (D) farming

24. **What is the name for the land that forms where a river flows into an ocean or another body of water?**
    - (F) glacier
    - (G) valley
    - (H) current
    - (J) delta

25. **The region of land along a river is a(n) _____ .**
    - (A) meander
    - (B) oasis
    - (C) floodplain
    - (D) riverbed

26. **About how long does it take the moon to travel the entire path around Earth?**
    - (F) one hour
    - (G) one day
    - (H) one month
    - (J) one year

27. **Tides occur because of the force between Earth and the moon, which is also known as _____ .**
    - (A) lunar pull
    - (B) inertia
    - (C) lunar orbit
    - (D) gravity

28. **In a lunar eclipse, Earth is between the moon and _____ .**
    - (F) a star
    - (G) the sun
    - (H) Mars
    - (J) Venus

29. **What would need to be found on a planet in order to verify that life as we know it was possible there?**
    - (A) oxygen
    - (B) hydrogen
    - (C) helium
    - (D) water

GO ON

30. Why do we only see one side of the moon from Earth?
   - (F) The moon does not rotate.
   - (G) The Earth's rotation is in sync with the moon's rotation.
   - (H) The moon's period of rotation is equal to its period of revolution.
   - (J) The Earth's rotation is equal to the moon's rotation.

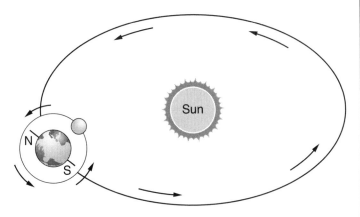

31. Which season would the Southern Hemisphere of Earth be experiencing in the diagram above?
   - (A) spring
   - (B) summer
   - (C) fall
   - (D) winter

32. The control center of a cell, which houses the cell's genetic material, is the _____ .
   - (F) mitochondrion
   - (G) cytoplasm
   - (H) cell membrane
   - (J) nucleus

33. Your body is made of many systems that control specialized functions. Which system is responsible for protecting organs and enabling movement?
   - (A) nervous
   - (B) circulatory
   - (C) muscular
   - (D) endocrine

34. All of the following are functions of the nervous system except _____ .
   - (F) receiving information
   - (G) responding to stimuli
   - (H) maintaining homeostasis
   - (J) preventing disease

35. Which is *not* a major source of energy for the body?
   - (A) fats
   - (B) carbohydrates
   - (C) DNA
   - (D) proteins

36. The heart is made of cardiac muscle. Which part of this muscle contracts to pump blood out of the heart?
   - (F) the atria
   - (G) the ventricles
   - (H) the aorta
   - (J) the septum

37. Which cells in the body fight disease?
   - (A) red blood cells
   - (B) white blood cells
   - (C) liver cells
   - (D) bone cells

38. Which small components of the respiratory system are responsible for the movement of oxygen through the blood?

    (F) bronchi

    (G) alveoli

    (H) nephrons

    (J) arteries

39 The eye is stimulated by light, which allows us to see objects. Which part of the eye allows light to enter?

    (A) the lens

    (B) the retina

    (C) the cornea

    (D) the pupil

40. A fertilized egg is called a(n) _____ .

    (F) zygote

    (G) chromosome

    (H) nucleus

    (J) ovary

41. Jeanette has brown hair and green eyes. What is the name for a segment of DNA that helps determine traits, such as brown hair and green eyes?

    (A) a chromosome

    (B) a nucleic acid

    (C) a gene

    (D) a ribosome

42. Which of these terms could be used to describe all animals?

    (F) producers

    (G) consumers

    (H) herbivores

    (J) carnivores

43. An ecosystem contains a large number of producers, consumers, and decomposers. The best way to represent the path energy takes as it is transferred from one organism to the next is in a food _____ .

    (A) chain

    (B) web

    (C) bank

    (D) source

44. In addition to their plant species, biomes differ most in their _____ .

    (F) altitude and distance from the equator

    (G) winds and humidity

    (H) temperature and precipitation

    (J) sunlight and storm frequency

45. If an area is inhabited by a large number of different species, it is said to be

    _____ .

    (A) extinct

    (B) biodiverse

    (C) populated

    (D) bioactive

46. Which is *not* a reason for the extinction of a species?

    (F) natural catastrophes

    (G) pollution

    (H) introduction of foreign species

    (J) captive breeding

STOP

Directions: Read the text below. Use information from the text to help you answer questions 1–4.

Miss Hopkins was conducting a science experiment for her class. The experiment instructed her to heat samples in a beaker of hot water. Miss Hopkins put water into a beaker and placed the beaker on a hot plate. The samples that she needed to heat were put in test tubes and placed into the beaker of water. After five minutes she removed the test tubes and told the class to observe any changes to the samples.

1. **Which of the following could Miss Hopkins have done to demonstrate lab safety to her students?**

   (A) perform other tasks while heating the tubes on the hot plate

   (B) remove her gloves before taking the tubes from the beaker

   (C) use tongs to remove the test tubes from the beaker of water

   (D) turn the hot plate on and then gather materials

2. **When Miss Hopkins removed the test tubes from the beaker of water, she noticed a small crack in the top of one of them. What should she do with this cracked tube?**

   (F) Throw it in the trash.

   (G) Continue using it until it breaks completely.

   (H) Lay it on the bench top and dispose of it later.

   (J) Dispose of it in a broken-glassware container.

3. **The next step of the experiment involves Miss Hopkins adding chemicals to the test tubes. What precautions can Miss Hopkins take to prevent a chemical spill?**

   _____

   _____

   _____

   _____

4. **What important steps should Miss Hopkins follow when the experiment is over?**

   _____

   _____

   _____

   _____

Grade 7

Directions: Read the questions. Choose the truest possible answer.

1. **Which of the following questions could a scientist try to answer through experimentation?**
   - (A) Do fish like to swim in fish tanks?
   - (B) Were dinosaurs afraid of people?
   - (C) Does more sunlight cause a flower to grow larger?
   - (D) Is it easier to play a guitar or a trumpet?

2. **An interpretation of an observation using both evidence and your own knowledge is a(n) _____ .**
   - (F) model
   - (G) fact
   - (H) hypothesis
   - (J) inference

3. **What testable prediction does a scientist try to answer through experimentation?**
   - (A) a fact
   - (B) a model
   - (C) a hypothesis
   - (D) a conclusion

4. **Which of the following describes a controlled experiment?**
   - (F) It contains only manipulated variables.
   - (G) All the variables are constant except one.
   - (H) It tests a scientific theory.
   - (J) The results do not support the hypothesis.

5. **Jacob wanted to see how the air pressure in his bicycle tires changed with temperature. What is the dependent variable in this experiment?**
   - (A) the bicycle tires
   - (B) the temperature
   - (C) the air pressure in the tires
   - (D) the height of the bicycle

6. **Which of the following *best* describes the next step in scientific inquiry if a hypothesis is not supported by an experiment?**
   - (F) adjust the hypothesis, and do an experiment to test it
   - (G) present the results as proof of the hypothesis
   - (H) repeat the experiment until it agrees with the hypothesis
   - (J) create a new experiment that will support the hypothesis

7. **What must happen before a hypothesis is accepted as a theory?**
   - (A) The hypothesis must be tested by one trial.
   - (B) The hypothesis must be tested by many trials.
   - (C) Many people must agree with the hypothesis.
   - (D) Many people must make similar predictions.

Grade 7

Directions: Read the text below. Use information from the text to help you answer questions 1–6.

Macy wanted to find out if hot water froze slower than room temperature water. She filled one ice cube tray with hot water and another ice cube tray with room temperature water. She put the trays into the freezer and checked them every hour to determine if ice had formed.

1. **The next step in Macy's experiment should be to _____ .**
   - (A) record her observations
   - (B) interpret her results
   - (C) draw a conclusion
   - (D) form a new hypothesis

2. **Before starting this experiment, Macy _____ that the hot water would take longer to freeze than the room temperature water.**
   - (F) recalled
   - (G) observed
   - (H) concluded
   - (J) predicted

3. **Why did Macy test both hot water and room temperature water?**
   - (A) It allowed her to state her results as a theory.
   - (B) It helped her form a hypothesis.
   - (C) It allowed her to make a valid comparison.
   - (D) It was easier to perform two tests.

4. **During Macy's experiment, the independent variable was the _____ .**
   - (F) volume of the water
   - (G) temperature of the water
   - (H) time that the water took to reach the freezing point
   - (J) freezing point of the water

5. **Name two ways in which Macy could present her data to the class.**

   _____

   _____

   _____

6. **What could Macy do to expand her experiment?**

   _____

   _____

   _____

STOP

Grade 7

Directions: Read the text below and study the diagrams. Use information from both to help you answer questions 1–5.

One afternoon, Dena and Lee were at the beach. As they walked along the beach, they noticed their footprints in the sand. The two girls decided to measure each other's footprints to see which were larger. They used a ruler that measured their footprints in centimeters.

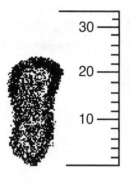

Dena's footprint   Lee's footprint

1. **In the picture above, how large is Lee's footprint?**
   - Ⓐ 1.9 cm
   - Ⓑ 15 cm
   - Ⓒ 19 cm
   - Ⓓ 23 cm

2. **How much larger is Dena's footprint than Lee's?**
   - Ⓕ 1 cm
   - Ⓖ 4 cm
   - Ⓗ 8 cm
   - Ⓙ 40 cm

3. **What is Dena's footprint size in decimeters?**
   - Ⓐ 2.3 dm
   - Ⓑ 23 dm
   - Ⓒ 230 dm
   - Ⓓ 2300 dm

4. **The girls' friend Elena was at the beach that day and measured her footprint as well. Elena's footprint is 2 centimeters smaller than Dena's. How long is Elena's footprint?**
   - Ⓕ 2 cm
   - Ⓖ 17 cm
   - Ⓗ 21 cm
   - Ⓙ 25 cm

5. **The girls want to measure the distance from their beach blankets to the water. If it takes them 10 steps to reach the water, what is a good estimate of the distance?**
   - Ⓐ 35 mm
   - Ⓑ 20 cm
   - Ⓒ 2 m
   - Ⓓ 10 km

STOP

Name_____ Date__

Directions: Study the diagram below. Use information from the diagram to help you answer questions 1–7.

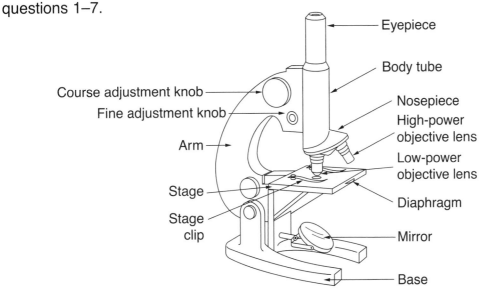

1. Penelope, a lab student, is using a microscope to observe a pond sample. Before she gets started, Penelope needs to move the microscope onto her lab bench. Which two parts of the microscope should she grasp in order to move it to her bench?

_____

2. Where should Penelope place the pond sample?

_____

3. Which part of the microscope will hold her sample in place?

_____

4. Through which part of the microscope should Penelope look in order to view her sample?

_____

5. Which part of the microscope controls the amount of light passing through the

   opening of the stage? _____

6. After her sample is in place, which part of the microscope should Penelope use to

   adjust the focus? _____

7. If Penelope wants to see the smallest objects in her sample, which lens should she use?

_____

Directions: Read the questions. Choose the truest possible answer.

1. Adrian wanted to measure 350 mL of water for an experiment. Which is the *best* piece of laboratory equipment to measure this liquid?
   - (A) a beaker
   - (B) a graduated cylinder
   - (C) a test tube
   - (D) a water dropper

2. Which tool would be *best* to use when trying to isolate and remove a tiny body part during a dissection lab?
   - (F) tweezers
   - (G) scissors
   - (H) scalpel
   - (J) forceps

3. Mrs. Taylor was demonstrating to her class how to boil approximately 500 mL of water in the laboratory using a hot plate. Which type of container should she put the water in?
   - (A) a beaker
   - (B) a graduated cylinder
   - (C) a test tube
   - (D) a spring scale

4. A spring scale relates the mass of an object to _____ .
   - (F) inertia
   - (G) momentum
   - (H) the force of Earth's gravity
   - (J) centripetal force

5. When preparing a wet-mount slide for the microscope, what is the *best* way to apply a drop of water to the specimen?
   - (A) pour the water from a graduated cylinder
   - (B) drop the water from a dropper
   - (C) hold the specimen under the water faucet
   - (D) dip the specimen into a beaker of water

6. When Kylie was measuring acid in a graduated cylinder, she noticed the surface of the acid was not level, but curved. What is this curved surface called?
   - (F) a conversion
   - (G) a meniscus
   - (H) an air bubble
   - (J) a milliliter

7. What is the magnification of an object if the eyepiece lens magnifies 10 times and the objective lens magnifies 40 times?
   - (A) 10 times
   - (B) 40 times
   - (C) 50 times
   - (D) 400 times

STOP

Grade 7

Directions: Study the diagram below. Use the diagram to help you answer questions 1 and 2.

1. Look closely at the diagram above. List three observations about what you see.

   _____

   _____

   _____

2. Use your observations to make an inference about the animals in the diagram.

   _____

   _____

Directions: Answer the following questions.

3. How do observations help scientists learn more about their surroundings? Be specific.

   _____

   _____

   _____

4. List some of the observations that you think might be made by a scientist who studies the weather.

   _____

   _____

   _____

Grade 7

Directions: Read the text below and study the table. Use information from both to help you answer questions 1–5.

Sylvia wants to see how high and low temperatures vary throughout the week. For five days in a row, she measures both the highest and the lowest temperature of the day. She takes her first two temperature readings on Monday and the final readings on Friday. She takes the thermometer readings in degrees Fahrenheit. Her data table for the temperature readings is shown below.

Temperature (degrees F)		
Day	Low	High
Monday	41	67
Tuesday	52	75
Wednesday	55	71
Thursday	42	64
Friday	50	68

1. **How is the information in the table organized?**

   _____

2. **Why is it important, especially when collecting many data points, to organize data effectively?**

   _____

   _____

3. **What is the best way for Sylvia to present her findings? Why?**

   _____

   _____

4. **What stages of scientific inquiry can occur once the data has been organized?**

   _____

   _____

5. **Using the information above, which day had the biggest difference between high and low temperatures?**

   _____

STOP

Directions: Read the text below. Use information from the text to help you answer questions 1–4.

Toby did an experiment to see how the speed of a toy car down a ramp would be affected by changing the angle of the ramp. He set up three ramps, each with a different angle. When he measured the angles of the ramps, Ramp 1 was 30°, Ramp 2 was 15°, and Ramp 3 was 45°.

Toby then put his toy car on each ramp. Using a stopwatch, he measured the time it took the car to go down it. He recorded his results.

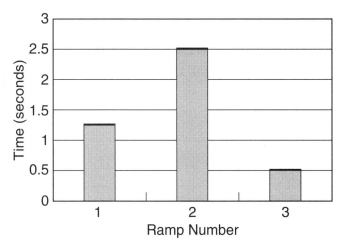

1. **Why was it important to use the same car on all three ramps?**

_____

_____

_____

2. **Which of the following statements is true?**

   (A) The car on Ramp 2 went down the ramp the fastest.

   (B) The car on Ramp 3 went down the ramp the fastest.

   (C) The car on Ramp 1 went down the ramp twice as fast as the car on Ramp 3.

   (D) The car on Ramp 2 went down the ramp twice as fast as the car on Ramp 1.

3. **What conclusion could Toby draw from this experiment?**

   (F) Toy cars travel at inconsistent speeds down ramps with different angles.

   (G) The greater the angle of the ramp, the slower the toy car's speed.

   (H) Toy cars travel the slowest on ramps with a small angle.

   (J) The angle of the ramp has no effect on the speed of the toy car.

4. **Why would it be too vague to draw the conclusion that increasing the angle of the ramp will increase the speed of the toy car?**

_____

_____

_____

STOP

Name_____ Date_____

Directions: Read the questions. Choose the truest possible answer.

Four different classrooms collected aluminum cans for a recycling project. Their goal was to collect 1,000 cans per classroom.

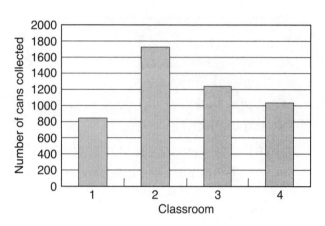

1. **Which of the following is the range of data shown in the bar graph?**
   - (A) 1 to 2000
   - (B) 812 to 1732
   - (C) 1 to 4
   - (D) 1038 to 1247

2. **Which classroom collected 1247 cans?**
   - (F) classroom 1
   - (G) classroom 1
   - (H) classroom 3
   - (J) classroom 4

3. **How many classrooms met their goal?**
   - (A) 0
   - (B) 1
   - (C) 2
   - (D) 3

The data table below shows the amount of five different types of fish found at a fish hatchery.

Type of Fish	Number of Fish
salmon	125
bass	582
catfish	477
perch	220
walleye	281

4. **How many more perch are at the hatchery than salmon?**
   - (F) 95
   - (G) 105
   - (H) 152
   - (J) 457

A class was surveyed on the number of siblings each student had. The circle graph below shows the results of this survey.

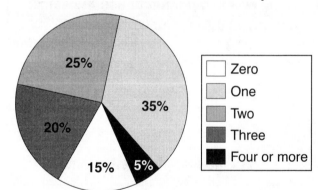

5. **If there were twenty students in the class, how many students had four or more siblings?**
   - (A) one
   - (B) two
   - (C) four
   - (D) eight

STOP

Name_____ Date_____

Directions: Read the text. Use information from the text to help you answer questions 1–4.

Derek and Hannah wanted to see what effect different amounts of table salt had on the boiling point of water. They measured 600 mL of water and divided it equally into three pans. The first pan contained no table salt. They added 10 g of table salt to the second pan and 20 g of table salt to the third pan. When the water in each pan began to boil, they recorded the highest temperature reading. They recorded their results in the table below.

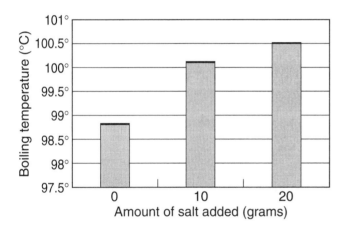

1. **Which pan was the control group for this experiment?**
   - (A) the pan with no salt
   - (B) the pan with 10 g of salt
   - (C) the pan with 20 g of salt
   - (D) no control group evident

2. **What was the independent variable in this experiment?**
   - (F) the amount of water added
   - (G) the temperature of the water
   - (H) the amount of salt added to the water
   - (J) the boiling point of the water

3. **What would be a good hypothesis for this experiment?**
   - (A) Adding salt to water prevents water from boiling.
   - (B) Adding more than 600 mL of water to the pan increases the boiling point of water.
   - (C) Increasing the amount of salt causes water to boil at a higher temperature.
   - (D) The boiling temperature of water increases when salt is removed from the water.

4. **What is a possible conclusion that Derek and Hannah could draw from this experiment?**
   - (F) Salt increases the boiling point of water.
   - (G) Salt decreases the boiling point of water.
   - (H) As more salt is added to water, the length of time it takes water to boil increases.
   - (J) The amount of salt in water has no relationship to the boiling point of water.

Directions: Read the questions. Choose the truest possible answer.

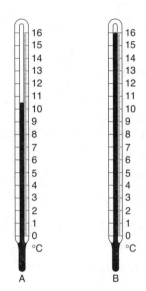

A   B

1. What is the temperature reading of thermometer A to the nearest half degree?

  (A) 10.0°C
  (B) 10.5°C
  (C) 11.0°C
  (D) 11.5°C

2. Kayla is doing an experiment in which she has to build a ramp with a 45° angle. In order to achieve this angle, Kayla must raise one side of a wooden board 33.5 cm. She is going to use a stack of textbooks to prop up the wooden board. When lying flat, the height of one textbook measures 4 cm. About how many textbooks can Kayla use without exceeding the desired height?

  (F) 6
  (G) 7
  (H) 8
  (J) 9

3. Jerome is performing an experiment in which he needs to measure 2.6 oz of a liquid. In his laboratory, Jerome has only a graduated cylinder, which measures volume in milliliters. Jerome knows that one ounce is equal to about 29 mL. About how many milliliters of liquid will Jerome need to equal 2.6 oz?

  (A) 35 mL
  (B) 55 mL
  (C) 75 mL
  (D) 95 mL

4. Tiara used a triple-beam balance to measure the masses of rock samples, and her results are shown below. Which is the best estimation of the total mass of the rock samples?

  Sample 1: 123.25
  Sample 2: 123.5
  Sample 3: 123.75
  Sample 4: 124.0

  (F) 400 g
  (G) 480 g
  (H) 600 g
  (J) 494.5 g

GO ON

Name_____   Date_____

Directions: Read the text below and study the diagram. Use information from both to help you answer questions 1–4.

Over 2,000 years ago, a Greek astronomer named Eratosthenes accurately measured the circumference of Earth by making observations and combining them with his geometry skills. While working in a library, Eratosthenes read about a deep vertical well located in the Egyptian city of Syene. He read that every year at noon on June 21st, the well was entirely lit up to the bottom with no shadow. This meant that the sun was directly over the city of Syene.

Eratosthenes then discovered that in Alexandria, a city approximately 925 km north of Syene, the sun cast a 7.2 degree shadow at noon on June 21st. Eratosthenes knew that the only way there could have been a shadow in Alexandria was if Earth were a sphere. This also led him to believe that Alexandria was 7.2 degrees away from Syene. He then had enough information to calculate the circumference of Earth.

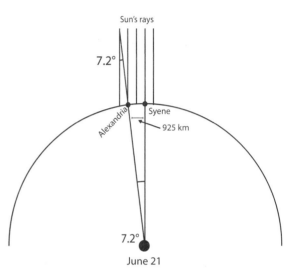

1. **In addition to time, what other two measurements did Eratosthenes use to calculate the circumference of Earth?**

   _____

   _____

2. **How many degrees are in a circle?**

   _____

   _____

3. **Using your answer from the previous question, what part of a circle is 7.2°?**

   _____

   _____

4. **Now you have enough information to solve for the circumference of Earth by multiplying the distance between Alexandria and Syene in kilometers and dividing by your answer to question 3. Be sure to use the correct units as you solve for the circumference. Use a separate sheet of paper for your calculations.**

   _____

   _____

Grade 7

Directions: Read the text below. Use information from the text to help you answer questions 1–5.

Density Investigation

During science class, Mrs. Davis showed her class a jar containing a golf ball floating in the middle of a volume of liquid. Mrs. Davis challenged her students to recreate the jar on their own. She provided each team of students with a jar, water, salt, and a golf ball. Althea, Calvin, and Matt noticed that when a golf ball was dropped into a jar of fresh water, it sank to the bottom. After noticing this, the group decided on a hypothesis. Then they began to perform trials. First, they mixed two teaspoons of salt into the fresh water. Then they placed the golf ball in the jar to see if it would float. If the ball did not float, they added more salt and performed another trial. The group continued in this manner until the golf ball floated on top of the liquid. Then they poured fresh water on top of the salt water in the jar. The golf ball remained in the middle of the jar. The group had figured out how to recreate the jar their teacher showed them!

1. **Write an appropriate hypothesis for Althea, Calvin, and Matt's investigation.**

   _____

   _____

2. **What scientific concept did Althea, Calvin, and Matt use in their investigation?**

   _____

   _____

3. **After performing the investigation once, what could Althea, Calvin, and Matt do next to confirm their results?**

   _____

   _____

4. **Write a conclusion to this investigation. Include an idea for further investigation into floating and sinking.**

   _____

   _____

   _____

   _____

   _____

   _____

   _____

   _____

   _____

   _____

GO ON

Grade 7

Directions: Read the text below. Use information from the text to help you answer questions 1–4.

Teana and George are discussing what happens when an object is dropped from a height. Teana thinks that all objects will fall at the same rate from the time they are dropped until they hit Earth's surface. George thinks that it is a little more complicated than that. He thinks that the mass of the object being dropped will have an impact on the rate at which it falls. They decide to perform an experiment to test the two hypotheses by dropping a variety of objects from a second story window, a height at which air resistance will have little impact on the results.

1. **What instruments will George use to measure the rate at which the objects fall?**

   _____

   _____

2. **Teana and George want to make a graph to present their results to the class. Which variables should go on the x-axis and the y-axis?**

   _____

   _____

3. **Teana thought that dropping only two objects from the window would provide enough information to draw a conclusion. George did not agree. He believed that dropping ten objects would allow them to draw a reliable conclusion. Whose method will give the best results? Why?**

   _____

   _____

   _____

4. **After performing this experiment, Teana forms a new hypothesis. She believes that the height at which an object is dropped has an impact on the rate at which it falls. How could Teana and George alter their experiment to test Teana's new hypothesis? In your answer, state what would be controlled and what would be tested in the experiment.**

   _____

   _____

   _____

   _____

   _____

   _____

   _____

STOP

Name_____ Date_____

Directions: Read the text below. Use information from the text to help you answer the essay question. Use a separate sheet of paper if needed.

Hybrid Cars

As concern increases about global warming and carbon dioxide levels in the atmosphere, scientists and engineers are seeking ways to reduce the amount of pollutants emitted into the atmosphere. Cutting back on the use of fossil fuels and using alternative energy sources will start to solve the problem. Hybrid cars, which are becoming more and more popular, provide a way to limit pollutants in the atmosphere.

Hybrid cars use a small gasoline-powered internal combustion engine, as well as a small electric engine. The battery for the electric engine is recharged by the gas engine, and therefore does not need to be plugged in to be recharged. These hybrid cars can go for 50 miles on a gallon of gas. Scientists and engineers are still working to develop an electric car that does not need a gas engine. Perhaps in the future we will not need to pull into a gas station to fill up our cars, and our atmosphere will be cleaner.

1.   **Scientists and engineers are working together to develop an electric car that does not need a gas engine. In an essay, describe two advantages of scientists and engineers working together to solve this problem. Explain how the invention of an electric car without a gas engine would help ease the concern about pollutants in the atmosphere.**

_____

_____

_____

_____

_____

_____

_____

_____

_____

_____

GO ON

Grade 7

Directions: Read the text below. Use information from the text to help you answer the questions.

Hurricane Prediction

Hurricane prediction has become more precise in recent years. In the past, meteorologists relied only on ships or airplanes to spot these powerful storms. Today, technology has advanced so that forecasters can accurately pinpoint when and where a hurricane will make landfall. In order to predict hurricanes, meteorologists use satellites that constantly monitor the areas of the ocean where hurricanes develop. When a hurricane forms, meteorologists use the satellite data to gather information about the wind speed in the hurricane and the speed and direction in which the hurricane is moving. This information can be put into a computer model, and the output will show the area where the hurricane will likely strike. As population increases in shoreline communities, it is more and more important to accurately predict the behavior of hurricanes.

Preparation can help reduce the damage caused by a hurricane. A family disaster plan and an emergency kit with a waterproof map of escape routes and refugee areas, food and water supplies, battery-powered radios and flashlights, and phone numbers, are important. Family members should keep the emergency kit nearby, move to higher ground, and evacuate when necessary. Having a plan can help family members deal with electrical problems, flooding, excessive garbage, bacteria and sewage in the water, insects, snakes, and other troubles that emerge during and after a hurricane. Reliable and accessible weather warning and transportation systems can also help to minimize hurricane damage.

1. **Describe two advantages of the new technology meteorologists use to predict hurricanes.**

    _____

    _____

    _____

2. **Propose a logical course of action to follow in the event of a flood.**

    _____

    _____

    _____

    _____

    _____

STOP

Grade 7

Directions: Study the table below. Use information from the table to help you answer questions 1–6.

Density of Some Substances	
Substance	**Density g/ml**
Rubbing alcohol	0.79
Glycerin	1.26
Corn Oil	0.93
Water	1.00
Wood	0.85
Aluminum	2.70
Rubber	1.34
Plastic	1.17
Cork	0.25

1. Anita created a density column in a graduated cylinder using the top four substances on the table above. Which liquid will settle to the bottom of the graduated cylinder?

   (A) water

   (B) corn oil

   (C) glycerin

   (D) rubbing alcohol

2. Which liquid in the above demonstration will remain at the top?

   (F) water

   (G) corn oil

   (H) glycerin

   (J) rubbing alcohol

3. If a piece of rubber were dropped into the density column, where would it settle in the column?

   (A) in the middle of the column with two liquids above and two liquids below

   (B) at the bottom

   (C) at the top

   (D) in the middle of the layer of water

4. Which liquid could be used to distinguish between cork and wood?

   _____

5. Which liquid could be used to distinguish between rubber and plastic?

   _____

6. Jamal has two samples of aluminum that are different sizes. What is the density of each sample? Explain.

   _____

   _____

   _____

   _____

STOP

Name_____   Date_____

Directions: Read the text below. Use information from the text to help you answer questions 1–4.

Talia and Jonas did an experiment to compare how the boiling point of water is changed when another substance is added to the water. In the first part of the experiment, they heated a beaker with 400 mL of water to its boiling point while taking temperature readings every two minutes. In the second part of the experiment, they stirred in sugar to 400 mL of water until no more would dissolve. Then they heated it to its boiling point while taking temperature readings every two minutes. The data from their experiment were used to make the graph below.

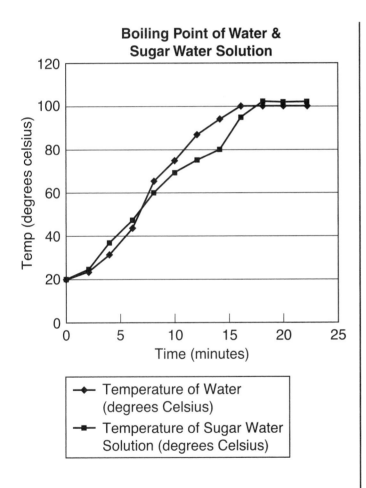

Boiling Point of Water & Sugar Water Solution

Legend:
- Temperature of Water (degrees Celsius)
- Temperature of Sugar Water Solution (degrees Celsius)

1. **What would be a good hypothesis for this experiment?**

    _____

    _____

2. **What inference could we make about the boiling point of soda using the data in the graph?**

    _____

    _____

3. **In the sugar water solution, which substance was the solute, and which substance was the solvent?**

    _____

    _____

4. **Write a conclusion for this experiment.**

    _____

    _____

    _____

STOP

Name_____ Date_____

Grade 7

Directions: Read the questions. Choose the truest possible answer.

1. Which of the following is a homogeneous mixture?
   - (A) sand
   - (B) saltwater
   - (C) sugar
   - (D) soapy water

2. Which of the following is a compound?
   - (F) sugar
   - (G) sulfur
   - (H) carbon
   - (J) chromium

3. Which of the following is a heterogeneous mixture?
   - (A) sand
   - (B) saltwater
   - (C) gold ring
   - (D) milk

4. Anthony is given a mixture of sand, salt, and iron filings. Anthony wants to remove the iron filings from the mixture. Which of the following physical properties will allow Anthony to remove the iron filings?
   - (F) solubility
   - (G) particle size and filtering
   - (H) magnetism
   - (J) boiling point

5. Anthony now wants to remove the salt from his mixture. Which of the following physical properties will allow Anthony to remove the salt?
   - (A) solubility
   - (B) particle size and filtering
   - (C) magnetism
   - (D) boiling point

6. A liquid with large particles is shaken until all the particles are dissolved into the liquid. This new substance is a(n) _____ .
   - (F) homogeneous mixture
   - (G) compound
   - (H) heterogeneous mixture
   - (J) element

STOP

0-7696-8067-4—Science Test Practice

Name_____ Date_____

Directions: Read the text below and study the equation. Use information from both to help you answer questions 1–7.

Dani mixes hydrochloric acid and calcium carbonate. Reactions occur and the products are carbon dioxide gas, calcium chloride, and water.

$$2HCl + CaCO_3 \Rightarrow CaCl_2 + H_2O$$

1. How many different elements are involved in this chemical reaction?

_____

2. Which compounds are the reactants?

_____

_____

3. How many atoms of oxygen are in the compound calcium carbonate?

_____

4. How many atoms of chlorine are in the compound calcium chloride?

_____

5. What is the name of this compound: $MgSO_4$?

_____

6. Name the elements present in the above compound.

_____

_____

7. During a chemical reaction, a chemical change takes place. Explain what happens in a chemical change.

_____

_____

_____

_____

STOP

Name_____ Date_____

Directions: Read the questions. Choose the truest possible answer.

1. Mercury, hydrogen, lithium, and sodium are all examples of _____ .
   - (A) elements
   - (B) solutions
   - (C) compounds
   - (D) mixtures

2. Which of these is a compound?
   - (F) Na
   - (G) Fe
   - (H) Pb
   - (J) O_2

3. A mixture that is uniform in composition is called a(n) _____ .
   - (A) element
   - (B) solution
   - (C) suspension
   - (D) compound

4. When electrons are transferred from one atom to another they form a _____ bond.
   - (F) molecule
   - (G) covalent
   - (H) ionic
   - (J) solution

5. The chemical formula for table sugar is $C_{12}H_{22}O_{11}$. How many atoms are in one molecule of table sugar?
   - (A) 45 atoms
   - (B) 12 atoms
   - (C) 3 atoms
   - (D) 11 atoms

6. When an atom loses an electron it becomes _____ .
   - (F) positive
   - (G) neutral
   - (H) negative
   - (J) suspended

7. Of the following, which pair of elements would share their electrons to form a molecular bond?
   - (A) sodium and chlorine
   - (B) oxygen and hydrogen
   - (C) potassium and iodine
   - (D) aluminum and sulfur

8. A given liquid has distinguishable particles that are not uniformly distributed throughout the liquid. This liquid is classified as a _____ .
   - (F) suspension
   - (G) solvent
   - (H) solution
   - (J) compound

9. Which one of the following is not a mixture?
   - (A) chocolate milk
   - (B) vinegar
   - (C) sand
   - (D) mud

Name_____ Date_____

Directions: Study the table below. Use information from the table to help you answer questions 1–3.

The Periodic Table of the Elements is an organized way of displaying the elements based on their physical and chemical properties.

	Group 1																	Group 18
Period 1	1 H Hydrogen 1.00794	Group 2																2 He Helium 4.0026
Period 2	3 Li Lithium 6.941	4 Be Beryllium 9.0122										Group 13	Group 14	Group 15	Group 16	Group 17		
													5 B Boron 10.811	6 C Carbon 12.011	7 N Nitrogen 14.0067	8 O Oxygen 15.9991	9 F Fluorine 18.9984	10 Ne Neon 20.183
Period 3	11 Na Sodium 22.9898	12 Mg Magnesium 24.305	Group 3	Group 4	Group 5	Group 6	Group 7	Group 8	Group 9	Group 10	Group 11	Group 12	13 Al Aluminum 28.9815	14 Si Silicon 28.086	15 P Phosphorus 30.97	16 S Sulfur 32.06	17 Cl Chlorine 35.455	18 Ar Argon 39.948
Period 4	19 K Potassium 39.098	20 Ca Calcium 40.08	21 Sc Scandium 44.956	22 Ti Titanium 47.87	23 V Vanadium 50.942	24 Cr Chromium 51.996	25 Mn Maganese 54.94	26 Fe Iron 55.845	27 Co Cobalt 58.9382	28 Ni Nickel 68.69	29 Cu Copper 68.546	30 Zn Zinc 65.39	31 Ga Gallium 69.72	32 Ge Germanium 72.59	33 As Arsenic 74.92	34 Se Selenium 78.96	35 Br Bromine 79.91	36 Kr Krypton 83.80
Period 5	37 Rb Rubidium 85.47	38 Sr Strontium 87.62	39 Y Yttrium 88.906	40 Zr Zirconium 91.22	41 Nb Niobium 92.906	42 Mo Molybdenum 95.94	43 Tc Technetium 96.91	44 Ru Ruthenium 101.07	45 Rh Rhodium 192.2	46 Pd Palladium 106.4	47 Ag Silver 107.868	48 Cd Cadmium 112.41	49 In Indium 114.82	50 Sn Tin (Stannum) 121.75	51 Sb Antimony 121.75	52 Te Tellurium 127.60	53 I Iodine 126.90	54 Xe Xenon 131.29
Period 6	55 Cs Cesium 132.905	56 Ba Barium 137.33	57–71* Lanthanides	72 Hf Hafnium 178.49	73 Ta Tantalum 180.948	74 W Tungsten 183.84	75 Re Rhenium 186.2	76 Os Osmium 190.2	77 Ir Iridium 192.2	78 Pt Platinum 195.08	79 Au Gold 196.967	80 Hg Mercury 200.59	81 Tl Thallium 204.18	82 Pb Lead 207.7	83 Bi Bismuth 208.98	84 Po Polonium (210)	85 At Astatine (210)	86 Rn Radon (222)
Period 7	87 Fr Francium (223)	88 Ra Radium (226)	89–103** Actinides	104 Rf Rutherfordium (261)	105 Db Dubnium (262)	106 Sg Seaborglum (266)	107 Bh Bohrium (267)	108 Hs Hasslum (265)	109 Mt Meitnerium (268)	110 Ds Darmstadtium (269)	111 Rg Roentgenium (272)	112 Uub Ununbium (277)	113 Unt Ununtrium	114 Uuq Ununquadium	115 Uup Ununpentium	116 Uuh Ununhexium	117 Ununseptium	118 Ununoctium

	57 La Lanthanum 138.91	58 Ce Cerium 140.12	59 Pr Prasseodymium 140.908	60 Na Neodymium 144.24	61 Pm Promethium (145)	62 Sm Samarium 150.36	63 Eu Europlum 151.96	64 Eu Gadollnlum 157.25	65 Tb Terblum 158.925	66 Dy Dysproslum 162.50	67 Ho Holmium 164.990	68 Er Herblum 167.26	69 Tm Thullum 168.934	70 Yb Yttarbium 173.04	71 Lr Lutetlum 174.97
*LANTHANIDES															
**ACTINIDES	89 Ac Actinium (227)	90 Th Thorium 232.038	91 Pa Protactinium 231.036	92 U Uranium 238.03	93 Np Nepyunium (237)	94 Pu Plutonium (244)	95 Am Americlum (243)	96 Cm Curium (247)	97 Bk Berkellium (247)	98 Cf Californium (251)	99 Es Einsteinium (252)	100 Fm Fermlum (257)	101 Md Mendelevlum (258)	102 No Nobelium (259)	103 Lr Lawrenclum (262)

1. What two characteristics do all elements share?

_____

_____

2. What are the two main categories of elements on the periodic table?

_____

_____

3. What type of information can be found about each element on the periodic table?

_____

_____

_____

STOP

Grade 7

Directions: Read the text below. Use information from the text to help you answer questions 1–6.

Trevor and Mariah were asked to set up an experiment demonstrating each of Newton's three laws of motion. They were given two Hall's carts, two inclines, a stopwatch, and a variety of masses.

To demonstrate the first law of motion, Trevor placed different masses in the two carts. He put one cart at the top of the first incline, and the other cart at the top of the second incline. Then he gave the carts an equal push down the inclines. Trevor then recorded his results.

1. **What does Newton's first law of motion state?**

   _____

   _____

   _____

2. **What would be an appropriate hypothesis for the first part of the lab demonstrating the first law of motion?**

   _____

   _____

   _____

3. **Why was it necessary for Trevor to give the carts an equal push down the incline?**

   _____

   _____

   _____

4. **How would increasing the amount of mass in each cart affect the inertia of the carts as they rolled across the floor?**

   _____

   _____

5. **Why did the carts eventually come to a stop?**

   _____

   _____

   _____

   _____

6. **How does the fact that the carts came to a stop explain Newton's first law of motion?**

   _____

   _____

   _____

GO ON

Directions: Read the text below. Use information from the text to help you answer question 7.

To test the second law of motion, Mariah suggested that they use a different amount of force on each cart while keeping the mass in each cart the same. In order to determine the velocity of the carts, they used the stopwatch to time how long it took for the carts to travel the 10 m across the floor. They pushed cart 2 harder than they pushed cart 1. Mariah and Trevor collected the following data: Cart 1 reached the 10-meter line in 4 seconds, and cart 2 reached the 10-meter line in 3 seconds.

7. **Calculate the velocity of each cart during the time it traveled 10 m. Be sure to use the correct units.**

_____

_____

Directions: Read the text below. Use information from the text to help you answer questions 8–9.

To test Newton's third law of motion, the students decided to use one cart and a cinderblock wall. They put the cart on the floor facing the wall. They then pushed the cart so that it crashed into the wall.

8. **Draw and label arrows on the pictures to show which is the action force and which is the reaction force.**

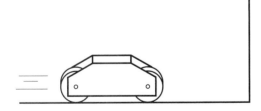 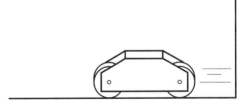

9. **Do these action-reaction forces cancel each other out? Explain your answer.**

_____

_____

STOP

Grade 7

Directions: Read the questions. Choose the truest possible answer.

1. What is the net force needed to accelerate a 32 kg wagon at 5 m/s²?
   - (A) 6.4 N
   - (B) 27 N
   - (C) 37 N
   - (D) 160 N

2. Julio and Luis have to move a box containing a 35 kg television from one room of their house to another. Julio has the ability to push with a force of 250 N while Luis can only push with a force of 100 N. If both boys pushed the box in the same direction with all the force they could, what would be the net force on the box, assuming no friction?
   - (F) 250 N
   - (G) 350 N
   - (H) 100 N
   - (J) 150 N

3. A baseball is rolling down a ramp with a velocity of 20 m/s. At the bottom of the ramp, the ball rolls onto fine-grained sand paper. Which of these is the best prediction of the ball's speed a few seconds after it rolls onto the sand paper?
   - (A) 0 m/s
   - (B) 10 m/s
   - (C) 20 m/s
   - (D) 30 m/s

4. The same baseball is rolled down the ramp again. At the bottom of the ramp, the ball rolls onto fine-grained sandpaper. This causes the ball's acceleration to slow down. The name given to the action of the sand on the ball is _____ .
   - (F) rolling friction
   - (G) fluid friction
   - (H) sliding friction
   - (J) kinetic friction

5. Bernadette attaches an 8 N weight to a spring. The spring stretches to 4 cm with this weight hanging from it. What would the new length of the spring be if a 12 N weight were used instead of the 8 N weight?
   - (A) 12 cm
   - (B) 10 cm
   - (C) 8 cm
   - (D) 6 cm

6. A boat is moving east at a speed of 20 km/hr. The wind is blowing from the west at 7 km/hr. Give the speed and direction of the boat.
   - (F) 13 km/hr east
   - (G) 27 km/hr east
   - (H) 13 km/hr west
   - (J) 27 km/hr west

STOP

Grade 7

Directions: Read the text below. Use information from the text to help you answer questions 1–4.

Energy Transfers

If you have ever skied downhill, then you have not only experienced a thrill, but you have also been a part of the physics of energy transformation.

From the time the skier gets on the ski lift, a number of important energy conversions begin to occur. A chain working the ski lift exerts a force on the skier that moves her up a large hill. The mechanical energy from the chain is doing work on the skier. The mechanical energy from the lift is then converted into potential energy in the skier.

On the top of the hill, the skier has a large amount of gravitational potential energy, which is the potential energy associated with the skier's position in relation to gravity. This potential energy depends on the mass of the skier, the height of the hill, and the force of gravity acting on the skier. As the skier descends the hill, the potential energy associated with the height of the hill transforms into kinetic energy, the energy of motion. Kinetic energy depends on the mass of the object and the speed at which it is traveling. As the skier plunges down the hill, she loses height and potential energy and gains speed and kinetic energy.

In order to stop, the skier digs her skis into the snow. This causes friction between the skis and the snow, which causes another energy conversion. Even after the ride for the skier has come to an end, the energy surrounding the skier continues to transform.

1. **Which form of energy is related to the speed of a skier down the hill?**
   - (A) kinetic energy
   - (B) potential energy
   - (C) thermal energy
   - (D) electrical energy

2. **When a skier stops at the bottom of a ski slope, friction causes the skier's kinetic energy to be transformed into**
   _____ .
   - (F) potential energy
   - (G) thermal energy
   - (H) electrical energy
   - (J) mechanical energy

3. **At the beginning of the passage, the ski lift carries the skier up the hill. The skier is said to _____ the lift.**
   - (A) gain energy from
   - (B) lose energy to
   - (C) provide energy to
   - (D) share energy with

4. **If a skier has a mass of 50 kg, what is the skier's potential energy at the top of a 35-meter hill?**

   _____

   _____

   _____

STOP

Name_____ Date_____

Directions: Study the concept map below and fill in the blanks with words from the Word Bank.

Heat is thermal energy. It can be transferred from one object to another. It always flows from an object with a high temperature to an object with a lower temperature.

Word Bank

| weather | gases | radiation | vacuum | liquids | convection |

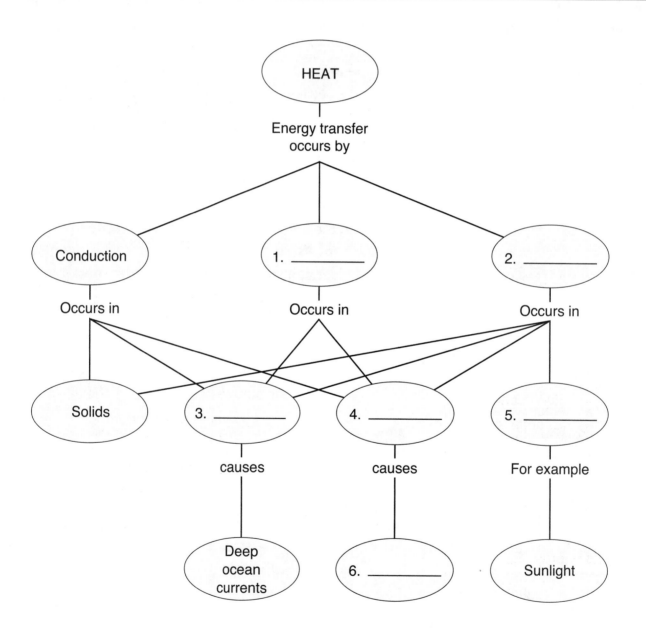

Grade 7

Directions: Study the diagram below. Use information from the diagram to help you answer questions 1–5.

The Electromagnetic Spectrum

Increasing frequency

Hz

Radio
Microwaves
Infrared light
Visible light
Ultraviolet light
X-rays
Gamma rays

M

Increasing wavelength

1. In which form does the energy from light travel?

- (A) electric waves
- (B) sound waves
- (C) luminescent waves
- (D) electromagnetic waves

2. A wave in the electromagnetic spectrum of light can be described by its energy, wavelength, and

_____ .

- (F) frequency
- (G) mass
- (H) size
- (J) polarity

3. Which of the following components of the electromagnetic spectrum has the shortest wavelength?

- (A) radio waves
- (B) microwaves
- (C) X-rays
- (D) gamma rays

4. The frequency of a wave is inversely proportional to its wavelength. In general, if a wave has a high frequency, then its

_____ .

- (F) wavelength is long
- (G) wavelength is short
- (H) speed is fast
- (J) speed is slow

5. A wave's frequency is proportional to its energy. Which type of wave has the greatest energy?

- (A) a radio wave
- (B) a microwave
- (C) a visible wave
- (D) an X-ray

STOP

Name_____ Date_____

Directions: Study the diagrams below. Use information from the diagrams to help you answer questions 1–5.

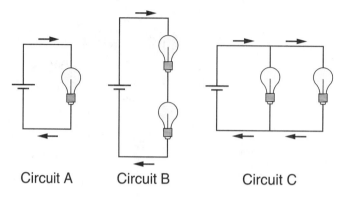

Circuit A   Circuit B   Circuit C

Ω **(Omega) = ohms**

1. The arrows in all three circuits indicate the flow of _____ .

    (A) protons
    (B) neutrons
    (C) electrons
    (D) photons

2. Which circuit diagram shows the light bulb(s) connected in series?

    (F) Circuit A
    (G) Circuit B
    (H) Circuit C
    (J) none of the above

3. The light bulbs in the circuits represent resistors. What is the best description of a resistor?

    (A) an object that increases the charge of electrons
    (B) an object that can reverse the flow of electrons
    (C) an object that does not affect the flow of electrons
    (D) an object that slows down the flow of electrons

4. Which circuit would still work if a light bulb was disconnected from the circuit?

    (F) Circuit A
    (G) Circuit B
    (H) Circuit C
    (J) none of the above

5. In Circuit B, if both light bulbs had a resistance of 50 Ω, what is the total resistance of the circuit?

    (A) 0.1 Ω
    (B) 1 Ω
    (C) 50 Ω
    (D) 100 Ω

STOP

Grade 7

Directions: Read the text below. Use information from the text to help you answer questions 1–6.

The sun has been producing energy for billions of years. Almost all of the energy on Earth begins with the sun, whether directly or indirectly. Plants convert the sun's radiant energy into chemical energy through the process of photosynthesis. This energy is not only used to fuel the plant's processes, but processes of other organisms as well. Solar energy, through the use of photovoltaic cells, can be directly converted into electrical energy. In recent years, solar energy has become a significant energy source for many of our energy needs.

1. Plants use the process of photosynthesis to produce energy. What are the products of photosynthesis?

_____

_____

2. How do the products of photosynthesis store energy?

_____

_____

3. Coal, petroleum, and natural gas are fossil fuels. Why can we say that the energy obtained by burning fossil fuels originated with the sun?

_____

_____

_____

4. Solar energy may provide much of the fuel we will need in the future. Why is this so?

_____

_____

_____

5. What are some drawbacks or limitations of solar energy?

_____

_____

_____

_____

6. List some objects that you use or know of that are powered by solar energy through photovoltaic cells.

_____

_____

_____

STOP

Name_____   Date_____

Directions: In the box below, draw the structure of an animal cell. Then label the nucleus, the cytoplasm, and the cell membrane.

1.

Directions: Read each question. Write your answers on the lines provided.

2. **What is the main job of the nucleus?**

_____

_____

3. **How does the cell membrane work to protect the cell?**

_____

_____

4. **Why are mitochondria called the energy centers of the cell?**

_____

_____

5. **What type of structure is the cytoplasm?**

_____

_____

6. **How would a plant cell differ from the cell you drew?**

_____

_____

_____

_____

_____

Name_____ Date_____

Grade 7

Directions: Read the questions. Choose the truest possible answer.

1. What is the basic unit of structure and function of an organism?
   - (A) tissue
   - (B) nucleus
   - (C) cell
   - (D) organ

2. Which of the following is *not* multicellular?
   - (F) a tree
   - (G) a worm
   - (H) a human
   - (J) a bacterium

3. What is the clear, jelly-like substance within a cell that contains the cell's organelles?
   - (A) nucleus
   - (B) cytoplasm
   - (C) chloroplast
   - (D) mitochondria

4. Which of the following is the *most* complex?
   - (F) cell
   - (G) organ
   - (H) tissue
   - (J) organ system

5. What is the term that means 'the body's tendency to keep an internal balance, or equilibrium'?
   - (A) stress
   - (B) fight or flight
   - (C) homeostasis
   - (D) feedback loop

6. Which of the following is *not* an example of an organism reacting to a stimulus?
   - (F) a frog floating in a pond
   - (G) a worm moving toward a light source
   - (H) a bacteria getting rid of excess water
   - (J) a girl eating food when she becomes hungry

STOP

Directions: Read the questions. Choose the truest possible answer.

1. **Mitosis occurs because a cell** _____ .
   - (A) has too many chromosomes
   - (B) has too few chromosomes
   - (C) has grown too large
   - (D) is too small

2. **What is the result of mitosis?**
   - (F) A cell maintains its size.
   - (G) A cell grows in size.
   - (H) A cell produces two daughter cells.
   - (J) A cell dies.

3. **Before mitosis occurs, the chromosomes** _____ **so that each new cell receives one copy of the chromosome.**
   - (A) replicate
   - (B) intercolate
   - (C) migrate
   - (D) translate

4. **During the anaphase of mitosis,** _____ .
   - (F) the nuclear membrane disappears
   - (G) all the chromosomes line up in the center of the cell
   - (H) the chromosomes are pulled to the ends of the cell
   - (J) the cell membrane pinches in two and divides the cytoplasm

5. **In which phase of mitosis do spindle fibers form?**
   - (A) interphase
   - (B) prophase
   - (C) metaphase
   - (D) anaphase

6. **The cells produced in mitosis contain** _____ .
   - (F) only one chromosome
   - (G) twice as many chromosomes as the parent cell
   - (H) one-third the number of chromosomes as the parent cell
   - (J) the same number of chromosomes as each other

7. **Most cells in our body divide by mitosis, although the** _____ **cells use a process called meiosis.**
   - (A) brain
   - (B) heart
   - (C) liver
   - (D) sex

8. **How do mitosis and meiosis differ?**
   - (F) Meiosis produces chromosome pairs, while mitosis does not.
   - (G) Mitosis produces chromosome pairs, while meiosis does not.
   - (H) Meiosis produces one cell from replication, while mitosis does not.
   - (J) Mitosis produces one cell from replication, while meiosis does not.

STOP

Name_____   Date_____

=========================== **Grade 7** ===========================

Directions: Read the text below. Use information from the text to help you answer questions 1–4.

Muscle

What allows basketball players to run around the basketball court, jump in the air, and score a winning shot? Every movement we make—jumping, smiling, even pumping blood through our bodies—requires muscles. Muscle is a tissue, meaning an assembly of cells that have similar characteristics and that perform a corresponding function together in the body.

There are four types of tissue that are found in the human body—muscle tissue, connective tissue, nerve tissue, and epithelial tissue. Voluntary muscles, ones that contract under our control, are at work in the basketball player's legs. They propel him into the air. These skeletal muscles are attached to his bones by tendons. Many organs in the body are controlled by involuntary muscles, which are also at work in the basketball player. Cardiac muscle contracts to circulate blood to every part of his body. Smooth muscle in his stomach contracts to help digest the food he consumed, which will later become a source of energy for the player. These involuntary muscles help the organs work together to perform their necessary function in the body.

1. **What is tissue?**
    - (A) an individual cell that works to perform a particular function in the body
    - (B) a group of cells that work together to perform the same function
    - (C) an individual organ that works to perform a particular function in the body
    - (D) a group of organ systems that work together to perform the same function

2. **The basketball player's muscles _____ , allowing him to jump into the air.**
    - (F) duplicate
    - (G) replicate
    - (H) expand
    - (J) contract

3. **The four types of tissue are connective, muscle, epithelial, and _____ tissue.**
    - (A) voluntary
    - (B) involuntary
    - (C) nerve
    - (D) smooth

4. **The tissue in the human body assembles to form _____ .**
    - (F) cells
    - (G) organs
    - (H) organ systems
    - (J) organisms

Name_____ Date_____

Directions: Read each statement below. Write T if the statement is true and F if it is false. If the statement is false, replace the underlined word with a word from the Word Bank to make the statement true.

```
┌─────────────── Word Bank ───────────────┐
│   brain      voluntary       muscles     │
│   tissues    organ system    stomach     │
│   heart      bones           lungs       │
│   enzymes    involuntary     organs      │
└──────────────────────────────────────────┘
```

_____ 1. Cells make up tissue, and tissue makes up a body's <u>organism</u>.

         _____

_____ 2. The <u>nerve</u> is an organ in the circulatory system that is made of four different kinds of
         tissue. _____

_____ 3. The <u>enzymes</u> in the stomach cause the chemical breakdown of food.

         _____

_____ 4. <u>Blood vessels</u> are part of the system that supplies blood throughout a person's body.

         _____

_____ 5. The muscles in both the stomach and the heart are <u>cardiac</u> muscles.

         _____

_____ 6. The organ in the nervous system that sends a signal to the leg muscles telling a
         person to jump is the <u>heart</u>. _____

_____ 7. Smooth muscle in the <u>stomach and small intestine</u> helps a person digest food to
         provide energy to the body. _____

_____ 8. The human <u>brain</u> contains marrow, produces blood cells, and provides support for the
         body. _____

_____ 9. Each organ in the body is part of a(n) <u>muscle</u> that performs a major function in the
         body, such as circulating blood or digesting food. _____

STOP

Name_____ Date_____

Directions: Read the questions. Choose the truest possible answer.

1. The nucleic acid of a virus is stored in the _____ .
   - (A) flagella
   - (B) cytoplasm
   - (C) mitochondria
   - (D) envelope

2. The chromosomes of bacteria are located in the _____ .
   - (F) cytoplasm
   - (G) flagella
   - (H) ribosome
   - (J) envelope

3. Which system is primarily responsible for protecting us from harmful bacteria and organisms?
   - (A) the circulatory system
   - (B) the respiratory system
   - (C) the immune system
   - (D) the endocrine system

4. T cells identify foreign_____ , which are marker molecules located on each pathogen.
   - (F) antigens
   - (G) antibodies
   - (H) lymphocytes
   - (J) phagocytes

5. Antibiotics are most effective on which pathogens?
   - (A) bacteria
   - (B) viruses
   - (C) fungi
   - (D) protists

6. The body's general defense mechanism, which involves the release of a number of chemicals and cells that fight the invading pathogen, is referred to as the _____ .
   - (F) immune response
   - (G) disease response
   - (H) pathogen destroyer
   - (J) phagocyte invader

7. The skin, breathing passages, and stomach are also included in the body's defense mechanism against infection because they _____ .
   - (A) provide a route of entry for pathogens
   - (B) provide a barrier to pathogens
   - (C) produce antibodies against pathogens
   - (D) produce hormones that resist infections

STOP

Name_____ Date_____

═══════════ **Grade 7** ═══════════

Directions: Read the text. Use information from the text to help you answer questions 1–2.

In some circumstances, asexual reproduction is beneficial for producing new organisms. Asexual reproduction eliminates the recombination of genes, which would produce offspring genetically different from the parent. Asexual reproduction results in offspring that have only the characteristics of the one parent. If a parent plant has adapted well to an environment, asexual reproduction ensures that the new organism will be just as suited to the environment as the parent.

1. **Strawberry plants grow along the ground and produce horizontal stems that grow into the soil surface. How is this an example of asexual reproduction?**

_____

_____

_____

_____

2. **Why would asexual reproduction in plants be important to farmers and gardeners?**

_____

_____

_____

_____

Directions: Study the concept map below. Use words from the Word Bank to fill in the lettered spaces below that correspond to the letters in the concept map.

─── Word Bank ───

budding	identical	plants	one parent
diverse	asexual	reproduction	

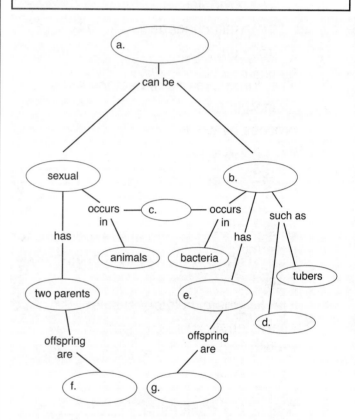

3. a. _____

    b. _____

    c. _____

    d. _____

    e. _____

    f. _____

    g. _____

STOP

Name_____ Date_____

Directions: Read the statements below and fill in the blanks with words from the Word Bank for 1–8. For 9–12, use the words to fill in the missing stages of the human life cycle.

─────────────── **Word Bank** ───────────────

| adolescent | labor | egg | infant | ovaries | testosterone |
| placenta | chromosomes | puberty | reproduction | zygote | embryo |

1. The _____ is the female sex cell.

2. _____ is the process by which living things produce new individuals of the same type.

3. During fertilization, 23 _____ from each parent, male and female, combine to determine the new organism's inherited characteristics.

4. The hormone that controls physical characteristics in men, such as facial hair growth and the ability to produce sperm, is _____ .

5. The female organs that produce egg cells are the _____ .

6. The _____ allows the exchange of nutrients, oxygen, and waste between the mother and the embryo.

7. The three stages of childbirth are _____ , delivery, and afterbirth.

8. The period of development in which the body becomes able to reproduce is _____ .

Human Life Cycle Stages

9. _____

10. _____

fetus

11. _____

child

12. _____

adult

STOP

Name_____ Date_____

Directions: Read the text below. Use information from the text to help you answer the question.

Bang! The starting pistol signals the start of a marathon, and Ashvin begins to run. During this marathon, Ashvin's organ systems will perform many tasks to maintain homeostasis. For example, running causes his body to produce a lot of carbon dioxide very quickly. To maintain a safe level of carbon dioxide in the blood, Ashvin breathes faster so he can get rid of that extra carbon dioxide.

1. **On the lines below, explain how Ashvin's organ systems help maintain homeostasis as he runs a marathon. Be sure to name the organ system, and explain what it does and why. Discuss at least three organ systems in your response.**

_____

_____

_____

_____

_____

_____

_____

_____

_____

_____

_____

_____

_____

STOP

Grade 7

Directions: Read the text below. Use information from the text to help you answer 1–9.

The Blueprint of Life

One Saturday afternoon, Janie was waiting at home for a visit from her Aunt Judy, whom she hadn't seen in three years. Suddenly, the doorbell rang. "It must be Aunt Judy," Janie thought.

When the door opened, there stood Aunt Judy. "Hello, Janie!" said Aunt Judy, pausing for a moment. "My, with your blonde, curly hair, you look just like Grandma Nancy!"

How is it possible that Janie could resemble one of her ancestors?

We are all born with a blueprint in our DNA that influences many of our traits, such as how we look and even the height to which we will grow. These traits are influenced by specific regions of DNA, called genes, which are passed on to us by both of our biological parents.

Genes are located on chromosomes, which are found in pairs. There are usually hundreds of genes in one chromosome. Because there are pairs of chromosomes, there are pairs of genes. Genes code for characteristics, and most genes code for more than one version of a characteristic. For example, one gene for hair can code for curly hair, and another for straight hair. The versions of the genes are called alleles—in this case, the curly allele and the straight allele. Each of your biological parents passed along one of his or her genes to you. Your pairs of genes may resemble your father in some ways and your mother in others.

If you inherit a gene pair with two straight hair alleles, you will have straight hair. But if you inherit one straight hair allele and one curly hair allele, you will have curly hair. This is because curly hair is the dominant trait. Janie must have inherited a curly hair allele from at least one of her parents. On the other hand, blond hair is a recessive trait, so Janie must have a blond hair allele from each parent.

In the early 1990s, scientists began the Human Genome Project, which was a large collaborative effort to map the over the 20,000 genes that make up the entire human genome. Understanding the human genome, which is the assembly of all the DNA of humans, can help us understand how we look or what size we will become. Even more importantly, it can help us prevent thousands of disorders and diseases that are carried by genes.

GO ON

Name_____ Date_____

Directions: Use words from the Word Bank to complete the statements.

─────────────── **Word Bank** ───────────────

| chromosomes | dominant allele | allele | heredity | pairs | dominant |

1. _____ is the transmission of traits from both biological parents to their offspring.

2. Janie's curly hair is determined by a particular _____ that contains the information for her curly hair trait.

3. Genes are located on _____ , which are made up of DNA and protein.

4. All of your chromosomes are found in _____ .

5. A(n) _____ is one of two or more versions of a gene for a particular trait.

6. If a particular trait, such as curly hair, always shows up in an organism with at least one allele for it, it is a(n) _____ trait.

Directions: Read the questions. Choose the truest possible answer.

7. If an individual has both a dominant and a recessive allele for a particular trait, then_____ .
   - (A) the recessive trait will show
   - (B) the dominant trait will show
   - (C) a mix of the recessive and dominant trait will show
   - (D) the trait will not be inherited

8. Because the gene for blond hair is recessive, what must be true of Janie's parents?
   - (F) Both have an allele for blond hair.
   - (G) Neither has an allele for blond hair.
   - (H) Only one has an allele for blond hair.
   - (J) Both have an allele for curly hair.

9. What is the main goal of the Human Genome Project?
   - (A) to distinguish between a learned trait and an inherited trait
   - (B) to determine which genes determine our physical appearance
   - (C) to determine the location of all the genes on human chromosomes
   - (D) to determine the location of the chromosomes in the body

Grade 7

Directions: Read the questions. Choose the truest possible answer.

1. **Which of the following is *not* true about adaptations?**

   (A) They can help an organism live longer.

   (B) They can help an organism reproduce.

   (C) Learned behavior is not considered an adaptation.

   (D) A helpful adaptation at one time may be harmful at another.

2. **A characteristic that is passed on from our biological parents through our DNA is _____ .**

   (F) a learned behavior

   (G) an inherited trait

   (H) a known trait

   (J) genetic diversity

3. **Inherited behavior in animals that is characteristic of a particular species and known without being taught is often referred to as the animal's _____ .**

   (A) genes

   (B) instinct

   (C) training

   (D) knowledge

4. **Which of the following dog behaviors is a learned behavior?**

   (F) barking at small animals

   (G) playing with its tail

   (H) playing dead

   (J) chewing on a bone

5. **Which of the following is true about imprinting?**

   (A) Imprinting can be changed over time.

   (B) Imprinting occurs in some bird species only.

   (C) Imprinting keeps young animals close to their mothers.

   (D) Imprinting occurs only between animals of the same species.

6. **Humans have the ability to use insight learning, which is _____ .**

   (F) solving a problem by applying prior knowledge

   (G) continuing to practice a skill until it is mastered

   (H) learning to recognize and follow the first moving object seen

   (J) learning to connect a stimulus with a good or bad event

7. **Ivan Pavlov, a Russian scientist, trained dogs to salivate at the sound of a bell. This training is known as _____ .**

   (A) instinct

   (B) imprinting

   (C) insight learning

   (D) conditioning

STOP

Grade 7

Directions: Read the text below and fill in the blanks with words from the word bank.

Word Bank

adaptation	desert	biotic factors	biome	energy
species	climate	habitat	niche	abiotic factors

All the living and nonliving things that interact in a specific area are known as the ecosystem. The size of an ecosystem may vary, and the surrounding ecosystems may blend into one another. An ecosystem is smaller than a **1.** _____ , which is characterized by the climate and the dominant life forms present in the area.

The **2.** _____ is the weather patterns that are observed in an ecosystem over a large period of time, and it includes both the temperature and the amount of precipitation in an ecosystem. Each animal **3.** _____ , or group of similar organisms that mate and produce offspring, has its own climate requirements. For example, polar bears and penguins are suited to life on ice in a frigid climate. Alternatively, an organism such as a scorpion can survive in a **4.** _____ , which is a biome that receives only 25 cm or less of rain each year. Through **5.** _____ , these animals can survive these extreme environmental conditions.

The living organisms that interact with each other in the ecosystem are the **6.** _____ , and the nonliving things, such as the sun, water, and air, are the **7.** _____ in the ecosystem. The specific location where an organism lives, which includes where it seeks food, rest, shelter, and escape from predators, makes up the organism's **8.** _____ factors.

An organism has a specific role within its natural habitat that determines its relations with other organisms. The food an organism eats and the manner in which that organism gets its food are both part of the organism's role. The role an organism plays in an ecosystem is called its **9.** _____ . When organisms eat one another, **10.** _____ flows through the ecosystem. Therefore, the relationship between all organisms is important to maintain the variety of species and the productivity of an ecosystem.

STOP

Name_____ Date_____

Directions: Read the questions. Choose the truest possible answer.

1. **Where does the energy for almost all ecosystems originate?**
   - Ⓐ from the producers
   - Ⓑ from the consumers
   - Ⓒ from the soil
   - Ⓓ from the sun

2. **All first-level consumers are _____ .**
   - Ⓕ herbivores
   - Ⓖ carnivores
   - Ⓗ omnivores
   - Ⓙ scavengers

3. **Consumers, organisms that depend on producers for food, are also known as**

   _____ .
   - Ⓐ scavengers
   - Ⓑ autotrophs
   - Ⓒ heterotrophs
   - Ⓓ decomposers

4. **The role of the decomposer is to**

   _____ .
   - Ⓕ provide all the food in an ecosystem
   - Ⓖ convert the energy from the sun into useful energy
   - Ⓗ eat all third-level consumers
   - Ⓙ rid the ecosystem of waste and dead organisms

5. **A food web or a food chain is the movement of _____ through an ecosystem.**
   - Ⓐ bacteria
   - Ⓑ light
   - Ⓒ energy
   - Ⓓ organisms

6. **How does energy get transferred along the food chain, through the producer to the consumer?**
   - Ⓕ A consumer feeds on the organism behind it in the food chain.
   - Ⓖ A consumer feeds on an organism before it in the food chain.
   - Ⓗ A producer feeds on an organism before it in the food chain.
   - Ⓙ A producer feeds on the organism behind it in the food chain.

7. **How does a food chain compare to a food web?**
   - Ⓐ A food web is only one possible path of energy moving through the ecosystem.
   - Ⓑ A food chain is only one possible path of energy moving through the ecosystem.
   - Ⓒ A food chain is all of the possible paths of energy moving through all the world's ecosystems.
   - Ⓓ A food web is all of the possible paths of energy moving through all the world's ecosystems.

8. **Which level of organisms get the most energy out of the food they make or consume?**
   - Ⓕ producers
   - Ⓖ decomposers
   - Ⓗ first-level consumers
   - Ⓙ higher-level consumers

Grade 7

Directions: Below is a diagram of a marine food web. Place all the organisms in the food web into the correct category: decomposer, producer, first-level consumer, second-level consumer, or higher-level consumer.

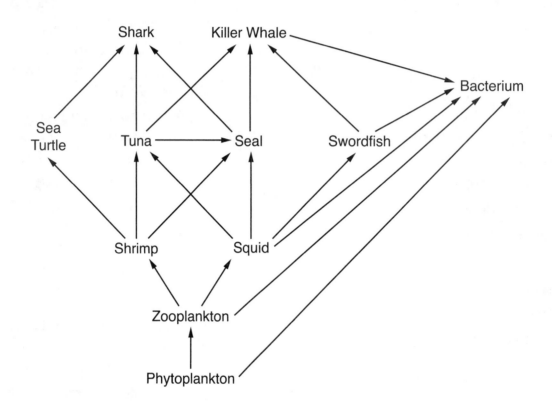

1. **Decomposer**

   _____

   _____

2. **Producer**

   _____

   _____

3. **First-Level Consumer**

   _____

   _____

4. **Second-Level Consumer**

   _____

   _____

5. **Higher-Level Consumer**

   _____

   _____

   _____

Grade 7

Directions: Read the questions. Choose the truest possible answer.

1. **Which of the following is a biotic factor?**
   - (A) soil
   - (B) rodent
   - (C) water
   - (D) rock

2. **Which of the following is an abiotic factor?**
   - (F) sunlight
   - (G) deer
   - (H) rodent
   - (J) grass

3. **Which of the following is an example of a biotic factor affecting an abiotic factor?**
   - (A) a duck bringing food to its duckling
   - (B) rivers providing drinking water for rodents
   - (C) a mountain blocking the wind from blowing
   - (D) deer waste and carcasses adding nutrients to the soil

4. **When might a particular abiotic factor be a limiting factor in an ecosystem?**
   - (F) if the quantity of the factor is in a limited supply
   - (G) if the factor is required by many of the organisms in the ecosystem
   - (H) if the ecosystem is at its carrying capacity
   - (J) all of the above

5. **In which biome would you expect to see the greatest species diversity?**
   - (A) desert
   - (B) temperate grassland
   - (C) tropical rainforest
   - (D) tundra

6. **Which abiotic factor would cause a deciduous tree in a temperate forest to lose its leaves in the winter?**
   - (F) water
   - (G) wind
   - (H) sunlight
   - (J) all of the above

STOP

Name _____ Date _____

Grade 7

Directions: Read the text below. Use information from the text to help you answer the essay question below.

A renewable resource can be naturally replaced quickly, a nonrenewable resource cannot be replaced, and an inexhaustible resource is available in a limitless supply. Since water is renewable, we may think we do not have to worry about losing it as a resource, but we do. Populations in arid regions, as well as in impoverished countries, are struggling to maintain an adequate water supply.

1. **In a short essay, describe three things that could lead to an inadequate water supply. Then discuss three things people can do to protect the water supply.**

_____

_____

_____

_____

_____

_____

_____

_____

_____

_____

_____

_____

_____

_____

_____

_____

STOP

Grade 7

Directions: Read the questions. Choose the truest possible answer.

1. **The role of an antigen in the human body is to**

    (A) cause disease.

    (B) make antibodies.

    (C) stimulate an immune response.

    (D) consume and digest viruses.

2. **Which organism is responsible for causing diseases in humans?**

    (F) B cell

    (G) Pathogen

    (H) Microphage

    (J) Killer T cell

3. **How do Helper T cells aid in the fight against sickness?**

    (A) They are proteins that attach to specific antigens.

    (B) They destroy infected cells so they can't replicate.

    (C) They "remember" how to make antibodies for particular diseases.

    (D) They recognize antigens and then activate B-cells and Killer T cells.

Directions: Read each question. Write your answers on the lines provided.

4. **What is the relationship between antigens and allergies?**

    _____

    _____

    _____

5. **What causes autoimmune diseases, and how are they different than other diseases?**

    _____

    _____

    _____

6. **How does your body prepare for a future attack by a virus it has fought before?**

    _____

    _____

    _____

STOP

Name_____ Date_____

Directions: Fill in the blanks with the correct word from the Word Bank.

```
──────── Word Bank ────────
washing your hands      alcohol
hygiene                 bad posture
stress                  exercise
sleep                   smoking
```

1. _____ is an important way to prevent the spread of sickness and disease.

2. _____ increases your heart rate, letting your body take in more oxygen.

3. _____ is a series of cycles in which your body regains its energy.

4. _____ is the negative physical and mental response to pressure.

5. _____ raises your chances of lung cancer and other diseases.

6. _____ puts strain on your muscles, which can lead to difficulty breathing.

7. _____ is the science of health and ways to maintain it.

8. _____ slows down the central nervous system.

Directions: Read the questions. Write your answers on the lines provided.

9. Stress is a common problem for many people. Why is this bodily response dangerous to your health?

_____

_____

_____

_____

10. Describe two ways in which you practice good hygiene in your daily life.

_____

_____

_____

_____

Name_____   Date_____

Grade 7

Directions: Read each question. Write your answers on the lines provided.

1. **What are calories, and why are they important to exercise and an active lifestyle?**

   _____
   _____
   _____
   _____

2. **Compare and contrast the two kinds of carbohydrates, simple and complex.**

   _____
   _____
   _____
   _____

Directions: Read the questions. Choose the truest possible answer.

3. **Why are fats important to a healthy diet?**
   - (A) They help with blood clotting.
   - (B) They build and repair your body.
   - (C) They strengthen bones and teeth.
   - (D) They store vitamins and provide energy.

4. **It is important to drink plenty of water because**
   - (F) water absorbs nutrients and carries away wastes.
   - (G) your body is about 70% water but does not need to be replenished.
   - (H) it keeps toxins in your system.
   - (J) the body's temperature does not need to be regulated.

5. **Calcium, Potassium, and Sodium are all examples of**
   - (A) fats.
   - (B) proteins.
   - (C) vitamins.
   - (D) minerals.

6. **Which of the following definitions describes the disorder known as anorexia nervosa?**
   - (F) when someone binge eats and then vomits in order to lose weight
   - (G) when someone starves himself or herself out of fear of gaining weight
   - (H) when someone eats only one kind of food and does not keep a balanced diet
   - (J) when someone eats too much food that is high in fat and low in other nutrients

STOP

Grade 7

Directions: Read each question. Write your answers on the lines provided.

1. Jackson and Desiree wanted to perform an experiment to study the behavior of earthworms. They wondered what an earthworm would do if it were removed from the soil and left in the sun. They placed an earthworm on the ground, and after one minute the earthworm had burrowed into the soil. Why is this behavior of the earthworm considered instinctual?

_____

_____

_____

2. The behaviors of many animals are tactics used for survival or for reproduction. Discuss one advantage and one disadvantage that the use of instinctual behaviors gives an animal.

_____

_____

_____

_____

_____

_____

_____

_____

3. Why do certain species of birds migrate in the winter? What must a bird be able to do in order to travel long migratory distances?

_____

_____

_____

_____

4. How can learning enhance a trait passed down by a parent? Give an example in your answer.

_____

_____

_____

_____

_____

_____

_____

_____

_____

STOP

Grade 7

Directions: Read each statement. Fill in the blank with the term that completes the sentence.

1. An adaptation is a trait used by an animal to _____ or _____ .

2. _____ adaptations are typical actions of a species.

3. An automatic response to a stimulus is called an _____ .

4. An action that becomes easier with practice is called a _____ .

5. A gosling will follow the first moving object it sees after it is born. This behavior is _____ .

Directions: Study the diagrams below. Then identify how the adaptation helps each bird species survive.

6. _____

_____

7. _____

_____

8. _____

_____

9. _____

_____

10. _____

_____

STOP

Name_____ Date_____

Directions: Study the diagram below. Use information from the diagram to help you answer questions 1–3.

This diagram shows the relationships among moisture, temperature, and plant species type.

Biomes

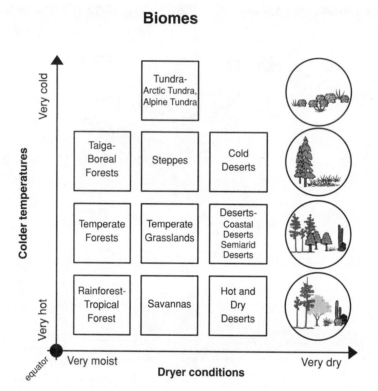

1. Which plant community in this diagram has adapted to hot and very dry conditions?

   Ⓐ savanna
   Ⓑ desert
   Ⓒ taiga
   Ⓓ thornwood

2. Which plant community is best suited for very cold and moderately moist conditions?

   Ⓕ tundra
   Ⓖ forest
   Ⓗ taiga
   Ⓙ grassland

3. Which statement *best* describes the relationship between temperature, moisture, and plant height?

   Ⓐ As temperature and moisture increase, plant height decreases.
   Ⓑ As temperature and moisture decrease, plant height increases.
   Ⓒ There is no relationship among temperature, moisture, and plant height.
   Ⓓ As temperature and moisture decrease, plant height decreases.

Name_____ Date_____

Directions: A species may become extinct for a number of different reasons. For items 1–4, explain how each occurrence could lead to the extinction of a species.

1. **Pollution**

    _____

    _____

    _____

2. **Competition**

    _____

    _____

    _____

3. **Limited habitats**

    _____

    _____

    _____

4. **Hunting**

    _____

    _____

    _____

Directions: Read each question. Write your answers on the lines provided.

5. Over geologic time there have been five mass extinctions of species living on Earth. Some people believe that Earth is going through another mass extinction now. Use the space below to suggest reasons for the mass extinctions of the past and, possibly, the present.

    _____

    _____

    _____

    _____

    _____

6. Sometimes human intervention can save a species from extinction. The Giant Panda feeds on a few species of bamboo, and if there is less bamboo the Giant Pandas are threatened. Once the bamboo flowers and sets seed, the plant dies. Sometimes, all the bamboo species flower at once, which threatens the food supply of the panda. Suggest a way to protect the panda's food supply.

    _____

    _____

    _____

    _____

    _____

STOP

Name_____ Date_____

Directions: Questions 1-10 are examples of different types of remains. Use the Word Bank to name the type of remain described.

Word Bank

trace fossil	cast	mold
index fossil	petrified remain	original remains

---

1. Imprint left behind after a snake slithered cross the sand millions of years ago

    _____

2. Rocklike wood from a tree that lived millions of years ago

    _____

3. Insect parts found in the fossilized sap of a pine tree

    _____

4. Rocklike remains of an organism that lived a short time in several parts of the world

    _____

5. A hollow depression from a dissolved bone found in a rock

    _____

6. Imprints left behind from a fern leaf

    _____

7. Animal footprints preserved in rock

    _____

8. A dinosaur bone lying in the sand

    _____

9. A shell-shaped mineral found in a rock cavity

    _____

10. Dinosaur tracks in a rock

    _____

STOP

Grade 7

Directions: Match each indicated layer of the earth with the correct term from the Word Bank.

┌─────────────────────────── **Word Bank** ───────────────────────────┐

   outer core   mantle   crust   inner core

└──┘

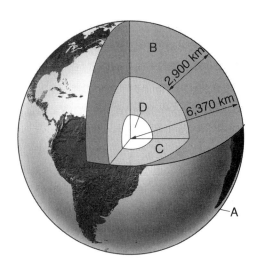

1. A _____

   B _____

   C _____

   D _____

Directions: Provide the name of the layer from the word bank that is best associated with the descriptions provided below.

2. Composed of solid iron and nickel

   _____

3. Generates Earth's magnetic field

   _____

4. Thickest under continents

   _____

5. The 'plastic-like" layer

   _____

6. The thickest layer

   _____

7. Made of molten iron and nickel

   _____

8. The densest layer

   _____

9. The outermost layer

   _____

10. The thinnest layer

   _____

STOP

Name_____ Date_____

Grade 7

Directions: Read each question. Write your answers on the lines provided.

1. Earthquakes are known to occur at plate boundaries. When an earthquake occurs at a transform-fault boundary, describe what happens to the tectonic plates to cause the earthquake.

   _____

   _____

2. An earthquake occurs at a convergent boundary of an oceanic plate and a continental plate. Describe what is occurring with the tectonic plates when the earthquake occurs.

   _____

   _____

3. Explain what occurs with two ocean plates at a divergent boundary during an earthquake.

   _____

   _____

4. What type of plate boundary is the San Andreas Fault? Which two plates are involved?

   _____

   _____

5. Describe how "stress" is involved in the creation of earthquakes.

   _____

   _____

STOP

Grade 7

Directions: Read the questions. Choose the truest possible answer.

1. A volcano that forms in the middle of a tectonic plate is called a(n) _____ .

   (A) hot spot
   (B) caldera
   (C) island arc
   (D) mid-ocean ridge

2. A volcano that forms at a convergent plate boundary between two oceanic plates is called a(n) _____ .

   (F) hot spot
   (G) caldera
   (H) island arc
   (J) mid-ocean ridge

3. Composite volcanoes, or stratovolcanoes, differ from shield volcanoes in that composite volcanoes _____ .

   (A) have a very broad shape
   (B) erupt fluid, basaltic lava
   (C) have steep walls
   (D) are made only of lava flows

4. Why is the boundary between the Pacific Plate and all the surrounding plates called the 'Ring of Fire'?

   (F) Many earthquakes occur there.
   (G) Hawaii is located in the center of the plate.
   (H) All of the world's active volcanoes are found there.
   (J) Many volcanoes are located at the convergent boundaries there.

5. Which best describes mid-ocean ridges?

   (A) They are convergent boundaries where magma rises up from the asthenosphere.
   (B) They are divergent boundaries where magma rises up from the asthenosphere.
   (C) They are transform-fault boundaries where magma rises up from the asthenosphere.
   (D) They are over mantle plumes where magma rises up from the asthenosphere.

6. The volcanic form created when a volcano erupts and collapses is called a _____ .

   (F) caldera
   (G) magma chamber
   (H) volcanic neck
   (J) cinder cone

7. Lava that is relatively high in silica is likely to be found in _____ .

   (A) flood basalts
   (B) shield volcanoes
   (C) divergent boundaries
   (D) composite volcanoes

STOP

Name_____ Date_____

Grade 7

Directions: Read the questions. Choose the truest possible answer.

1. **Weathering is a result of exposure of Earth materials to _____ .**
   - Ⓐ external processes at Earth's surface
   - Ⓑ external processes below Earth's surface
   - Ⓒ internal processes at Earth's surface
   - Ⓓ internal processes below Earth's surface

2. **The type of weathering that involves breaking a rock down without altering its chemical structure is _____ .**
   - Ⓕ hydrolysis
   - Ⓖ mechanical
   - Ⓗ chemical
   - Ⓙ oxidation

3. **When water gets into a crack in a rock and freezes, the water expands. When the water thaws, the rock breaks apart. This is called _____ .**
   - Ⓐ glacial drift
   - Ⓑ abrasion
   - Ⓒ ice wedging
   - Ⓓ jointing

4. **The form of weathering that occurs when Earth materials react with oxygen in the air is called _____ .**
   - Ⓕ acid rain
   - Ⓖ hydrolysis
   - Ⓗ carbonation
   - Ⓙ oxidation

5. **Chemical weathering is *most* common where the climate is _____ .**
   - Ⓐ warm and dry
   - Ⓑ warm and wet
   - Ⓒ cold and wet
   - Ⓓ cold and dry

6. **Which of the following is *not* an example of how living organisms can play a role in weathering?**
   - Ⓕ Birds nest in trees.
   - Ⓖ Lichens release acids, which break down rocks.
   - Ⓗ Small animals burrow and loosen rocks and soil.
   - Ⓙ Plant roots pry apart rocks.

7. **Which is *not* an agent of erosion?**
   - Ⓐ running water
   - Ⓑ clouds
   - Ⓒ wind
   - Ⓓ ice

8. **A wide, sloping deposit of sediment formed when a stream flows away from a mountain range is a(n) _____ .**
   - Ⓕ delta
   - Ⓖ flood plain
   - Ⓗ alluvial fan
   - Ⓙ drainage basin

9. **The slowest form of mass movement is a _____ .**
   - Ⓐ mudflow
   - Ⓑ slump
   - Ⓒ creep
   - Ⓓ landslide

STOP

Grade 7

Directions: Complete the diagram of a rock cycle below using words from the Word Bank.

Rock Cycle

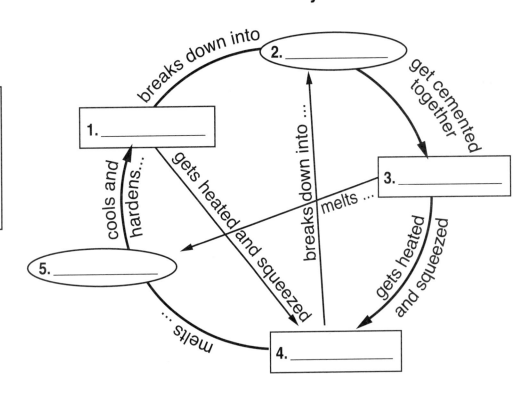

Word Bank

magma
sedimentary rock
sediments
igneous rock
metamorphic rock

Directions: Read each statement. Write your answer on the lines provided.

6. Rocks in this family are classified as clastic, chemical, or organic.

_____

7. Rocks in this family are classified as intrusive or extrusive.

_____

8. Rocks in this family are classified as foliated or nonfoliated.

_____

9. This family of rocks is associated with volcanoes.

_____

10. This family of rocks is associated with fossils.

_____

Name_____ Date_____

Directions: Read the passage below and study the graph. Use information from both to help you answer questions 1–4.

Devon, Jonas, Yumi, and Katie just finished learning about soils and how important they are to all living organisms. Their teacher asked the students to perform an experiment to test how well plants grow in different types of soil. They sprouted and grew bean plants in four different soil mixtures while controlling other variables that may affect plant growth (amount of water and sunlight). Below are the results of their experiment.

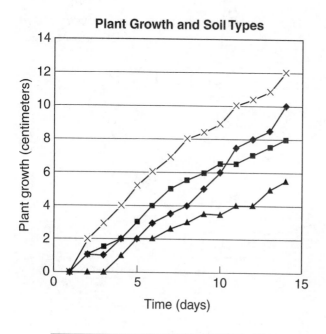

Plant Growth and Soil Types

Legend:
- ◆ Plant A (potting soil from a store)
- ■ Plant B (50% sand and 50% soil)
- ▲ Plant C (75% sand and 25% soil)
- ✕ Plant D (even mixture of sand, organic matter, and soil)

1. **Why do you think Plant C had the least amount of growth?**

_____

_____

_____

_____

2. **Look at the growth pattern of Plant A compared with Plant D. Describe the possible composition of the store-bought soil that Plant A grew in.**

_____

_____

_____

3. **Write a conclusion for this experiment.**

_____

_____

_____

4. **After their experiment, Yumi realized that they kept each plant in different rooms, each with a different temperature. What does this mean for their results?**

_____

_____

_____

_____

STOP

Grade 7

Directions: Read the questions. Choose the truest possible answer.

1. **What is the main source of energy for the water cycle?**
   - (A) the earth-moon system
   - (B) flowing water
   - (C) the sun
   - (D) gravity

2. **The process by which water vapor in the atmosphere changes into clouds is called _____ .**
   - (F) condensation
   - (G) transpiration
   - (H) evaporation
   - (J) precipitation

3. **The process by which plants give water vapor to the atmosphere is called _____ .**
   - (A) condensation
   - (B) transpiration
   - (C) evaporation
   - (D) precipitation

4. **What is the term given to water that does not soak into the ground or evaporate?**
   - (F) water table
   - (G) precipitation
   - (H) runoff
   - (J) groundwater

5. **Which of these contains most of Earth's fresh water?**
   - (A) oceans
   - (B) lakes and rivers
   - (C) glaciers
   - (D) groundwater

6. **Most evaporation takes place over _____ .**
   - (F) rivers
   - (G) lakes
   - (H) glaciers
   - (J) oceans

7. **The weather forecaster says there is a relative humidity of 100%. This means that _____ .**
   - (A) it is foggy
   - (B) it is raining
   - (C) the air has hardly any water vapor
   - (D) the air can not hold any more water vapor

8. **The dew point is the temperature at which air is saturated and _____ .**
   - (F) evaporation occurs
   - (G) condensation occurs
   - (H) precipitation occurs
   - (J) transpiration occurs

STOP

Grade 7

Directions: Read the questions. Choose the truest possible answer.

1. Air is a _____ .
   - (A) mixture
   - (B) compound
   - (C) element
   - (D) solution

2. Water vapor is added to the atmosphere primarily through _____ .
   - (F) condensation
   - (G) precipitation
   - (H) sublimation
   - (J) evaporation

3. Which atmospheric gas is a product of respiration and the burning of fossil fuels?
   - (A) oxygen
   - (B) nitrogen
   - (C) carbon dioxide
   - (D) argon

Directions: Read each question. Write your answers on the lines provided.

4. Name the gas that, when found in the stratosphere, protects us from harmful ultraviolet rays, but when found closer to Earth in the troposphere can be harmful.

   _____

5. What is the name of the bottom layer of the atmosphere? How does temperature change with altitude in this layer of the atmosphere?

   _____

   _____

   _____

6. How does temperature change with altitude in the stratosphere? Why?

   _____

   _____

   _____

7. As elevation increases in the atmosphere, air pressure does what?

   _____

8. What is the greenhouse effect? Is it harmful?

   _____

   _____

   _____

   _____

   _____

   _____

STOP

Grade 7

Directions: Read the questions. Choose the truest possible answer.

1. Which cloud type name means "layered"?
   - (A) cumulus
   - (B) stratus
   - (C) alto
   - (D) cirrus

2. A(n) _____ cloud is generally the first cloud type seen with the approach of a warm front.
   - (F) altocumulus
   - (G) nimbostratus
   - (H) cumulus
   - (J) cirrus

3. A(n) _____ cloud is also called a "thunderhead."
   - (A) altostratus
   - (B) cirrostratus
   - (C) cumulonimbus
   - (D) nimbostratus

4. Which type of cloud usually forms in fair weather?
   - (F) nimbostratus
   - (G) cumulonimbus
   - (H) cumulus
   - (J) altostratus

5. When an updraft causes ice particles to bounce around in a thunderhead cloud, which type of precipitation is formed?
   - (A) snow
   - (B) sleet
   - (C) freezing rain
   - (D) hail

6. Which of the following is not a way that water vapor is transported into the upper atmosphere to create clouds?
   - (F) cold air rising because of convection
   - (G) cold or warm air moving up a mountain range
   - (H) warm air rising because of convection
   - (J) warm or cold fronts pushing air up

7. What is the name for the ratio of the actual amount of water vapor in the air to the maximum amount of water vapor the air can hold at that temperature?
   - (A) relative humidity
   - (B) specific humidity
   - (C) absolute humidity
   - (D) extreme humidity

STOP

Grade 7

Directions: Read the questions. Choose the truest possible answer.

1. **Phytoplankton found in oceans remove which gas from the atmosphere?**
   - (A) nitrogen
   - (B) carbon dioxide
   - (C) oxygen
   - (D) water vapor

2. **Fish populations have decreased in the last 50 years mainly because of**
   _____ .
   - (F) overfishing
   - (G) competition with other species
   - (H) lack of food
   - (J) increase in ocean temperatures

3. **On average, how does the salinity of the Arctic Ocean in the winter compare to its salinity in the summer?**
   - (A) Salinity in the winter will be greater than summer.
   - (B) Salinity in the summer will be greater than winter.
   - (C) Salinity will remain constant throughout the year.
   - (D) Salinity will fluctuate unpredictably throughout the year.

4. **Ocean currents are mainly caused by**
   _____ .
   - (F) Earth rotating on its axis
   - (G) density differences and wind
   - (H) plate tectonics
   - (J) the moon's gravitational pull

5. **Hurricanes form over ocean water**
   _____ .
   - (A) near glaciers
   - (B) in the winter
   - (C) in the polar regions
   - (D) in the equatorial region

6. **Estuaries contain very sensitive ecosystems because living organisms there have adapted to _____ .**
   - (F) warm water
   - (G) fresh water only
   - (H) saline water only
   - (J) both fresh and saline water

7. **Ignoring local tide effects, how many low and high tides occur every day?**
   - (A) 1 low, 1 high
   - (B) 2 low, 1 high
   - (C) 1 low, 2 high
   - (D) 2 low, 2 high

8. **What percentage of Earth is covered by oceans?**
   - (F) 50%
   - (G) 71%
   - (H) 90%
   - (J) 97%

STOP

Name_____ Date_____

Directions: Fill in the blank with words from the Word Bank to complete the model of the solar system below.

--- **Word Bank** ---

Mercury	Mars	Earth	Pluto	asteroid belt	Venus
Neptune	Saturn	Sun	Uranus	Jupiter	

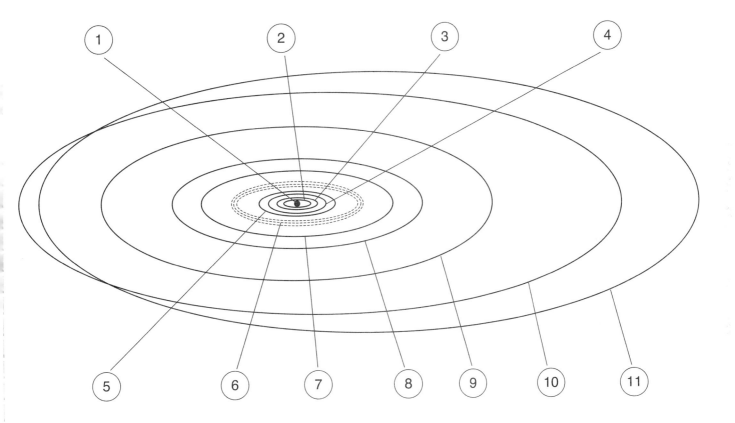

1. _____   7. _____

2. _____   8. _____

3. _____   9. _____

4. _____   10. _____

5. _____   11. _____

6. _____

STOP

Grade 7

Directions: Read each question. Write your answers on the lines provided.

1. Describe the shape and tilt of the orbits of the planetary objects in the solar system.

_____
_____
_____
_____

2. List the terrestrial planets. Describe the temperature and composition of the atmospheres of these planets. Explain how each planet's distance from the sun affects the temperature and atmosphere.

_____
_____
_____
_____
_____
_____
_____
_____
_____
_____

3. What are sunspots?

_____
_____
_____

4. How do solar flares create auroras?

_____
_____
_____
_____

5. What is the relationship of the speed of revolution of a planetary object to the position of the planetary object in the solar system?

_____
_____
_____
_____
_____
_____
_____

STOP

Directions: Read each question. Write your answers on the lines provided.

1. In reference to size and scale in the universe, rank the following celestial objects from smallest to largest: galaxy, solar system, star, planet, dwarf planet.

_____

_____

2. What is the name given to a group of stars that looks like an animal, an object, or a person?

_____

3. The North Star, or Polaris, is located in which constellation?

_____

4. What is the name given to the process that takes place in the core of stars, in which two hydrogen atoms become one helium atom?

_____

5. A massive star has a relatively short life span. At the end of its life it creates a large explosion called a(n)

_____ .

6. What are the three major types of galaxies?

_____

_____

7. A strong gravitational field from which even light cannot escape is called a(n)

_____ .

8. The color of a star reveals the
_____ of the star.

9. A cloud of interstellar gas and dust is called a(n)

_____ .

10. The distance that light travels in one year is called a(n) _____ .

11. Our home galaxy, the Milky Way, has a(n) _____ shape.

12. How does Earth's revolution affect the viewing of constellations?

_____

_____

_____

_____

STOP

Name_____   Date_____

Grade 7

Directions: Read each question. Write your answers on the lines provided.

1. How long does it take Earth to rotate once on its axis? How long does it take Earth to make a complete revolution around the sun?

   _____

2. The sun appears to rise in the east and set in the west. How is this related to the rotation of Earth? Explain.

   _____

   _____

   _____

3. If viewed from above the North Pole, does Earth rotate clockwise or counterclockwise?

   _____

4. How would the passage of one year be different for someone living in the Southern Hemisphere than in the Northern Hemisphere?

   _____

   _____

   _____

   _____

Directions: Read the questions. Choose the truest possible answer.

5. Complete the following sequence by filling in the missing moon phase: new, waxing crescent, 1st quarter,

   _____ .

   Ⓐ full
   Ⓑ 3rd quarter
   Ⓒ waning gibbous
   Ⓓ waxing gibbous

6. During which phase is the moon closest to the daytime path of the sun in the sky?

   Ⓕ full
   Ⓖ new
   Ⓗ 1st quarter
   Ⓙ 3rd quarter

7. Why do we only see one side of the moon from Earth?

   Ⓐ The moon's period of rotation is equal to its period of revolution.
   Ⓑ Earth's rotation is twice as fast as the moon's rotation.
   Ⓒ The moon does not rotate.
   Ⓓ Earth's rotation is equal to the moon's rotation.

8. During which phase does a lunar eclipse occur?

   Ⓕ new
   Ⓖ 1st quarter
   Ⓗ full
   Ⓙ 3rd quarter

STOP

     0-7696-8067-4—Science Test Practice

Name_____ Date_____

Directions: Study the table below. Use information from the table to help you answer questions 1–4.

Planet	X	Y	Z	Q
Mass	10^{45} km	10^{45} km	10^{24} km	10^{24} km
Radius	8,000 km	5,000 km	8,000 km	5,000 km

1. If you measured the weight of an object on Planet X, what would you also be measuring?

   _____

   _____

2. Would an apple weigh more on Planet X or Planet Z? Why?

   _____

   _____

   _____

   _____

3. Could you jump higher on Planet Y or Planet Q? Why?

   _____

   _____

   _____

   _____

4. Explain why an object has a different weight on Planet X than it does on Planet Y, even though the planets have the same mass. Remember that the force of gravity on an object depends on the distance from the object to the center of the planet.

   _____

   _____

   _____

   _____

   _____

   _____

STOP

Name_____ Date_____

Directions: Study the figure below. Use information from the figure to help you answer questions 1–2.

Group	14	15	16	17
	32	33	34	35
Period 4	**Ge**	**As**	**Se**	**Br**

1. The element selenium (Se) has an atomic number of _____ .
   - (A) 16
   - (B) 17
   - (C) 32
   - (D) 34

2. An element that lies in period 3, group 14 of the periodic table would have _____ .
   - (F) the same number of protons and electrons as Ge
   - (G) chemical and physical properties similar to those of Ge
   - (H) the same number of protons and electrons as Se
   - (J) chemical and physical properties similar to those of Se

Directions: Read the questions. Choose the truest possible answer.

3. When water is boiled, what happens?
   - (A) Water changes from an element to a compound.
   - (B) Water becomes a mixture.
   - (C) Water undergoes a physical change.
   - (D) Water undergoes a chemical change.

4. The hydrogen and oxygen _____ in a water molecule are held together by chemical bonds.
   - (F) atoms
   - (G) electrons
   - (H) nuclei
   - (J) mixtures

5. The tendency of an object at rest to stay at rest and an object in motion to continue moving is described by the law of _____ .
   - (A) friction
   - (B) momentum
   - (C) inertia
   - (D) gravity

6. The momentum of an object can be determined if the mass of an object is multiplied by its _____ .
   - (F) friction
   - (G) inertia
   - (H) velocity
   - (J) acceleration

7. Which of these is an example of the effect of gravity?
   - (A) A paperclip moves toward a magnet.
   - (B) A soccer ball slows down while rolling through grass.
   - (C) A race car speeds up when the drivers pushes the gas pedal.
   - (D) A baseball falls to the ground.

GO ON

Name_____ Date_____

Directions: Read the text below and study the table. Use information from both to help you answer questions 8–10.

Three students conducted an experiment to find out how increasing the amount of weight they carried while completing an obstacle course affected their speed through the course. They first completed the course without carrying weights. In the second and third trials, they carried 5- and 10-pound weights, respectively. Their data are shown in the table below.

	Time (seconds)	Time (seconds)	Time (seconds)
Student	No weight	+5 pounds	+10 pounds
Student One	35	38	40
Student Two	31	32	35
Student Three	42	43	46

8. **Which factor is the manipulated variable in this experiment?**
   - (F) the amount of weight carried in each trial
   - (G) the speed for each trial
   - (H) the weather for each trial
   - (J) the weight of each student in each trial

9. **Which of the following statements would make a reasonable hypothesis for this experiment?**
   - (A) Height is directly proportional to an individual's speed.
   - (B) Carrying additional weight while completing the obstacle course slows an individual down.
   - (C) Dressing improperly while completing an obstacle course slows an individual down.
   - (D) Weight will have no effect on an individual's performance.

10. **Based on the data in the table, which statement is accurate?**
    - (F) Student Two weighed the most out of all three students.
    - (G) Student One was slower than Student Three the first time through the obstacle course.
    - (H) Students One through Three were slowed down by the weight.
    - (J) Student Three was the quickest through the obstacle course.

GO ON

Name_____ Date_____

Directions: Read the questions. Choose the truest possible answer.

11. In the absence of friction, your gravitational potential energy at the top of the first hill of a roller coaster is

    _____ .

    (A) equal to your kinetic energy right before you reach the bottom of the hill

    (B) greater than your kinetic energy right before you reach the bottom of the hill

    (C) greater than your kinetic energy when the ride comes to a stop

    (D) equal to your kinetic energy when the ride comes to a stop

12. Light travels in what form?

    (F) electric waves

    (G) sound waves

    (H) electromagnetic waves

    (J) incident waves

13. Heat trapped in a greenhouse is an example of the transfer of heat by

    _____ .

    (A) insulation

    (B) friction

    (C) convection

    (D) conduction

14. At zero degrees on the Celsius scale, water _____ .

    (F) boils

    (G) freezes

    (H) evaporates

    (J) condenses

15. What net force is required to accelerate a 45-kg wagon at 3 m/s²?

    (A) 0.08 N

    (B) 15 N

    (C) 48 N

    (D) 135 N

16. What is the main function of the endocrine system?

    (F) It controls function and development of all parts of the body.

    (G) It removes pathogens.

    (H) It collects fluids.

    (J) It transports water and nutrients to all parts of the body.

17. What is the correct order for the components that constitute an organism, starting with the most basic unit?

    (A) organ system, organ, tissue, cell

    (B) cell, tissue, organ, organ system

    (C) tissue, cell, organ, organ system

    (D) organ, organ system, tissue, cell

GO ON

Name_____   Date_____

18. Which organ system contains the kidneys, the bladder, and the urethra?

- (F) the endocrine system
- (G) the digestive system
- (H) the immune system
- (J) the excretory system

19. Through the process of photosynthesis, plants _____ .

- (A) convert glucose into carbon dioxide and oxygen to produce energy
- (B) use their own energy to convert carbon dioxide and oxygen into water and carbon monoxide
- (C) use sunlight to convert carbon dioxide and water into oxygen and glucose
- (D) convert carbon dioxide into oxygen and protein to produce chlorophyll

20. A plant that can photosynthesize captures light from the sun in its _____ .

- (F) stem
- (G) cytoplasm
- (H) chloroplasts
- (J) roots

21. Sylvia has type O blood and brown eyes because of the _____ that both of her parents passed on to her.

- (A) hormones
- (B) genes
- (C) behaviors
- (D) antibodies

22. For Simon to receive a recessive trait from his parents, which of the following must be true?

- (F) Neither parent must carry the dominant allele.
- (G) Both parents must carry the recessive allele.
- (H) Only one parent has to carry the recessive allele.
- (J) Both parents must carry the dominant allele.

23. In the birth cycle, the zygote develops into the _____ .

- (A) embryo
- (B) fetus
- (C) infant
- (D) egg

24. Bacteria and viruses are different from each other in that _____ .

- (F) bacteria are pathogens, but viruses are not
- (G) viruses are pathogens, but bacteria are not
- (H) bacteria have all the genetic information they need to reproduce, but viruses do not
- (J) bacteria are visible under microscopes, but viruses are not

25. Which of the following behaviors would most likely be a learned behavior?

- (A) a lion cub pouncing on prey
- (B) a bird building a nest
- (C) a spider spinning a web
- (D) a young child riding a bike

Name_____ Date_____

=== **Grade 7 Posttest** ===

Directions: Study the figure below. Use information from the figure to help you answer questions 26-28.

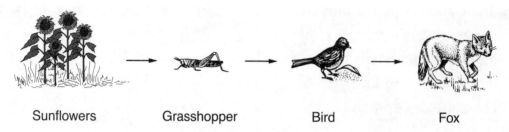

Sunflowers   Grasshopper   Bird   Fox

26. The figure above best represents a(n)
   _____ .
   - (F) food chain
   - (G) food web
   - (H) energy pyramid
   - (J) energy web

27. Which organism in the figure above is a first-level consumer?
   - (A) the sunflower
   - (B) the grasshopper
   - (C) the bird
   - (D) the fox

28. Which organism in the figure above receives the most available energy?
   - (F) the sunflower
   - (G) the grasshopper
   - (H) the bird
   - (J) the fox

Directions: Read the questions. Choose the truest possible answer.

29. Which of the following is not a renewable resource?
   - (A) the sun
   - (B) the wind
   - (C) coal deposits
   - (D) trees

30. Which of the following is least likely to lead to adaptation?
   - (F) stable climates
   - (G) new predators
   - (H) new landforms
   - (J) changing food supply

31. The upper mantle and the crust of Earth are collectively known as the
   _____ .
   - (A) exosphere
   - (B) biosphere
   - (C) hydrosphere
   - (D) lithosphere

32 The picture is an illustration of the water cycle. Letter B illustrates which process of the cycle?
   - (F) evaporation
   - (G) condensation
   - (H) precipitation
   - (J) collection

Name_____ Date_____

Directions: Study the figure below. Use information from the figure to help you answer questions 33-34.

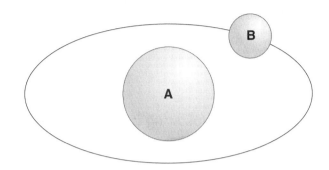

33. **If it takes B approximately 27 days to orbit A, what are A and B?**
  - Ⓐ A is the sun and B is Earth.
  - Ⓑ A is Earth and B is the sun.
  - Ⓒ A is Earth and B is the moon.
  - Ⓓ A is the moon and B is Earth.

34. **The position of B with respect to A causes _____ .**
  - Ⓕ moon phases
  - Ⓖ eclipses
  - Ⓗ tides
  - Ⓙ all of the above

Directions: Read the questions. Choose the truest possible answer.

35. **What causes day and night on Earth?**
  - Ⓐ Earth's revolution around the sun
  - Ⓑ the moon's revolution around Earth
  - Ⓒ solar and lunar eclipses
  - Ⓓ Earth's rotation on its axis

36. **Which statement most accurately explains why seasons occur?**
  - Ⓕ Earth is farther from the sun in the summer and closer to the sun in the winter.
  - Ⓖ Earth is farther from the sun in the winter and closer to the sun in the summer.
  - Ⓗ The tilt of Earth's axis as it moves around the sun results in seasons.
  - Ⓙ The movement of the moon around Earth causes seasons.

37. **Weather occurs in which layer of Earth's atmosphere?**
  - Ⓐ troposphere
  - Ⓑ stratosphere
  - Ⓒ mesosphere
  - Ⓓ thermosphere

38. **Clouds are composed mainly of _____ .**
  - Ⓕ dust and ozone
  - Ⓖ oxygen and helium
  - Ⓗ water and ice
  - Ⓙ hydrogen and helium

Page 9
1. B
2. F
3. D
4. G
5. D
6. G
7. C
8. F
9. C

Page 10
10. J
11. A
12. H
13. B
14. F
15. A

Page 11
16. H
17. D
18. G
19. A
20. H
21. D

Page 12
22. F
23. D
24. J
25. C
26. H
27. D
28. G
29. D

Page 13
30. H
31. B
32. J
33. C
34. J
35. C
36. G
37. B

Page 14
38. G
39. D
40. F
41. C
42. G
43. B
44. H
45. B
46. J

Page 15
1. C
2. J
3. Possible answer: Place chemicals on the lab bench in a way that reduces the chance of accidentally knocking over a container. Look around to make sure the chemicals are in view. Handle chemicals with care.
4. Clean up, return equipment, dispose of all items properly, make sure hot plate is turned off and unplugged, and wash her hands

Page 16
1. C
2. J
3. C
4. G
5. C
6. F
7. B

Page 17
1. A
2. J
3. C
4. G
5. a table or a chart
6. Possible answer: She could repeat the same experiment using different liquids, or she could test water against another liquid while keeping the temperature constant.

Page 18
1. C
2. G
3. A
4. H
5. C

Page 19
1. arm, base
2. stage
3. stage clips
4. eyepiece
5. diaphragm
6. coarse adjustment knob
7. high-power objective lens

Page 20
1. B
2. J
3. A
4. H
5. B
6. G
7. D

Page 21
1. Possible answer: The otter is wet. It is carrying a fish in its mouth. The otter and the bird are standing in shallow water.
2. Possible answer: Otters eat fish, but they do not eat birds.
3. Scientists can use information they gather to learn about the world. For example, observing animals in their habitats can help scientists learn about how the animals live.
4. Possible answer: temperature; amount of precipitation; cloud formations; signs of change in weather, such as thunderstorms.

Page 22
1. The information is arranged sequentially; high and low temperatures are separated.
2. When collecting many data points, the data may be confusing if the points aren't organized correctly.
3. a bar graph, so it is easy to compare the differences between all of the temperatures
4. Interpret data then draw conclusion
5. Monday

Page 23
1. A different-sized car would make the results inaccurate. The car needs to be a controlled part of the experiment, so that only ramp angle is measured.
2. B
3. H
4. As the angle of the ramp approaches 90 degrees, the car will no longer go down the ramp.

Page 24
1. B
2. H
3. D
4. F
5. A

Page 25
1. A
2. H
3. C
4. F

Page 26
1. B
2. H
3. C
4. G

Page 27
1. the angle of the sun, and the distance between Syene and Alexandria
2. 360°
3. 1/50th
4. 46,250 km

Page 28
1. If salt is dissolved in water, the golf ball will float.
2. differences in density of different materials
3. They could do the experiment over again.
4. Possible answer: The density of salt water is greater than that of fresh water. A golf ball has a density that is between salt water and fresh water and therefore floats between a layer of salt water on the bottom and fresh water on top. A further investigation might include mixing the two layers to see where the golf ball would rest, or using a material other than a golf ball to determine if the same amount of salt is needed to make the new object float as was needed to make a golf ball float.

Page 29
1. He will use the meter stick to measure distance and the stopwatch to measure time.
2. Mass is on the x-axis and the rate at which the object fell is on the y-axis.
3. George's idea to drop ten objects will give the best results. In scientific

experimentation, multiple trials are used to confirm results.

4. Use two or three different heights. Control: mass and shape or size of object. Tested: time, which is used to calculate speed.

Page 30

1. Possible answer: In recent years, scientists and engineers have begun to work together to develop ways to help make the atmosphere cleaner. The fact that scientists and engineers are working together will help save time in solving the problem. It also allows experts from different areas to come together and brainstorm. If the experts succeed in creating an electric car without a gas engine, the pollutants emitted into the atmosphere will be greatly reduced. This type of electric car would not need fossil fuels, which are harmful to the atmosphere.

Page 31

1. Possible answer: The new technology allows meteorologists to predict the hurricanes early and accurately. This gives people enough time to evacuate the area where the hurricane is scheduled to strike.
2. Possible answer: Store drinking water and emergency kit with you. Move to higher floors of home. Keep battery-operated radio on hand and follow instructions. If told to evacuate, do so and move to high ground. Avoid flooded areas, even in a car; keep a radio with you.

Page 32

1. C
2. J
3. B
4. Rubbing alcohol
5. Glycerin
6. The density of each sample is 2.70 g/mL. Since density is a physical property of a substance, it does not change when the size of the sample changes.

Page 33

1. Dissolved substances can change the boiling point of water.
2. Soda would have a similar boiling point to the sugar water solution.
3. Sugar is the solute, and water is the solvent.
4. As the data shows, dissolved substances change the boiling point of water.

Page 34

1. B
2. F
3. A
4. H
5. A
6. F

Page 35

1. 5
2. Hydrochloric acid and calcium carbonate
3. 3
4. 2
5. Magnesium sulfate
6. Magnesium, Sulfur, Oxygen
7. In a chemical change, new bonds form when old bonds between atoms break. A new substance is formed from two or more substances.

Page 36

1. A
2. J
3. B
4. H
5. A
6. F
7. B
8. F
9. B

Page 37

1. They cannot be broken down further, and they each have distinguishing properties.
2. metals and nonmetals
3. Answers will vary: Atomic mass, atomic number, number of electrons in the outer shell, size of the atom

Page 38

1. An object will stay in motion until acted upon by an unbalanced force.
2. The carts will remain in motion until acted upon by an unbalanced force.
3. Trevor's results would have been inaccurate if he had given the carts an unequal push.
4. The carts will have a greater amount of inertia.
5. The force of friction pushed the carts in the direction opposite to their movement.
6. Friction is an unbalanced force that caused the cart to stop.

Page 39

7. Cart 1 had an average velocity of 2.5 m/s. Cart 2 had an average velocity of 3.3 m/s.
8. Student should put one arrow over cart pointing toward wall labeled "action force" and another arrow on the wall pointing away from wall (toward cart) labeled "reaction force."
9. No, because the forces are acting on different objects. For example, when the cart hits the wall, one force is on the cart and the other force is on the wall.

Page 40

1. D
2. G
3. B
4. F
5. D
6. G

Page 41

1. A
2. G
3. A
4. 1750 J or 1.7 kJ

Page 42

1. convection
2. radiation
3. liquids
4. gases
5. vacuum
6. weather

Page 43

1. D
2. F
3. D
4. G
5. D

Page 44

1. C
2. G
3. D
4. H
5. D

Page 45

1. glucose and oxygen gas
2. Energy is stored as chemical energy in glucose.
3. Fossil fuels are made of dead plant and animal material from thousands of years ago. These plants produced food through photosynthesis, and the animals got energy from the sun by eating the plants.
4. It is renewable, or constant, unlike many of today's sources of fuel. It is environmentally friendly.
5. Possible answer: The sun doesn't shine all the time, solar energy cannot be stored, and it is expensive to produce and install collectors of solar energy.
6. Possible answers: heating home systems, calculators, cars, lights, etc.

Page 46

1. The outer circle should be labeled cell membrane, the inner space cytoplasm, and the center circle nucleus.
2. The nucleus is the control center of the cell. It houses DNA that directs cell activities.
3. It encloses the cell and its contents and lets only certain substances in and out.
4. Inside the mitochondria is where energy is transferred from glucose to a usable form (ATP).
5. a jelly-like substance
6. A plant cell contains a cell wall, chloroplasts, and large vacuoles.

Page 47

1. C
2. J
3. B
4. J
5. C
6. F

Page 48
1. C
2. H
3. A
4. H
5. B
6. J
7. D
8. F

Page 49
1. B
2. J
3. C
4. G

Page 50
1. organs
2. heart
3. true
4. true
5. involuntary
6. brain
7. true
8. skeleton
9. organ system

Page 51
1. D
2. F
3. C
4. F
5. A
6. F
7. B

Page 52
1. They produce independent plants from these stems.
2. They can maintain plants that have the characteristics they want.
3. a. reproduction; b. asexual; c. plants; d. budding; e. one parent; f. diverse; g. identical

Page 53
1. egg
2. Reproduction
3. chromosomes
4. testosterone
5. ovaries
6. placenta
7. labor
8. puberty
9. zygote
10. embryo
11. infant
12. adolescent

Page 54
Answers will vary, but should discuss three of the following organ systems: Respiratory system: Ashvin will breathe faster and deeper, to provide more oxygen for his body; Circulatory system: Ashvin's heart will pump harder and faster, allowing the cells in his body to receive more oxygen and nutrients, and get rid of wastes; Skin: Ashvin will begin to produce sweat, which will cool him down and maintain his temperature; Skeletal: Ashvin's skeleton will provide structural support and

absorb and distribute much of the impact he experiences as he runs, keeping his organs safe; Digestive: Ashvin's digestive system has already absorbed fats, proteins, and carbohydrates which he requires to fuel his running; Muscular: Ashvin's muscles assist the circulatory, respiratory, and digestive systems.

Page 56
1. Heredity
2. dominant allele
3. chromosomes
4. pairs
5. allele
6. dominant
7. B
8. F
9. C

Page 57
1. C
2. G
3. B
4. H
5. C
6. F
7. D

Page 58
1. biome
2. climate
3. species
4. desert
5. adaptation
6. biotic factors
7. abiotic factors
8. habitat
9. niche
10. energy

Page 59
1. D
2. F
3. C
4. J
5. C
6. G
7. B
8. F

Page 60
Decomposer: bacterium
Producer: phytoplankton
First-Level Consumer: zooplankton
Second-Level Consumer: squid, shrimp
Higher level Consumer: seal, swordfish, tuna, sea turtle, killer whale, shark

Page 61
1. B
2. F
3. D
4. J
5. C
6. J

Page 62
1. Answers will vary, but students may mention poor sanitation, pollution, overpopulation, and overuse. Ways to protect the water supply may include

installing cleaning or filtration systems, curbing pollution, setting limitations or bans on water use, and controlling the population in areas where fresh water is scarce.

Page 63
1. C
2. G
3. D
4. Possible answer: Antigens cause an immune system response. Allergies occur when the immune system reacts to antigens that are not harmful, such as pollen.
5. Possible answer: Autoimmune diseases are caused by the human body attacking its own cells. They are different than other diseases because the immune system mistakes its own cells to be pathogens.
6. The body has Memory B cells that "remember" how to make certain antibodies for viruses that the body has fought off in the past. This way, the recovery time is shorter.

Page 64
1. washing your hands
2. exercise
3. sleep
4. stress
5. smoking
6. bad posture
7. hygiene
8. alcohol
9. Possible answer: Stress can cause a person to lose sleep, and can also cause headaches and stomach aches.
10. Possible answer: Every morning I take a shower, where I wash my body and hair, and then I brush my teeth. I also make sure to wash my hands on a regular basis.

Page 65
1. Calories are how we measure the energy obtained from food. People with active lifestyles must take in more calories. Calories are used up during exercise, so they need to be replaced to stay healthy. Also, person who takes in many calories may need to exercise to avoid being overweight.
2. Simple carbohydrates are sugars, and they provide a quick source of energy; complex carbohydrates are made of many sugar molecules linked together, and provide long-lasting energy.
3. D
4. F
5. D
6. G

Page 66
1. To the earthworm, the light is the stimulus and moving away from the light is an unlearned response.
2. Possible answers: advantage: all animals within a species will have the same reproductive instincts and instincts allow organisms to survive when they can't think; disadvantage: another species may exploit the behavior of that species and affect the population.
3. Some species migrate to find a location with more food. To travel long distances, birds must store food energy as fat and navigate.
4. Many animals inherit characteristics that help them survive, but need to practice using the characteristics in order to become proficient. Student answers for examples may vary, but may include walking, running, climbing, fighting, flying, hunting, building, etc.

Page 67
1. reproduce, survive
2. behavioral
3. instinct
4. learned behavior
5. imprinting or instinct
6. drills into trees for food
7. gets nectar from flowers
8. cracks seeds
9. wades in water and mud without sinking in
10. grasps prey

Page 68
1. B
2. F
3. D

Page 69
1. An increase in the death rate because of a change in conditions can wipe out the population or wipe out the breeding adults; less genetic diversity allows for less adaptation.
2. A new species can enter an area and outcompete the resident species in its niche.
3. Some species have very restricted diets or require a large area. As resources dwindle, the species dies out.
4. Some species have been overhunted by humans.
5. Possible answer: changes in Earth's geology (shift in Earth's plates, meteorite impact) and changes in climate (warming or cooling, too wet, or too dry). Answers may vary for the present, but may suggest clear-cutting of rain forests, climate change, abundance of hunting, loss of habitat, etc.
6. Possible answer: creating corridors of wild land between bamboo forests so Giant Pandas can move to other areas when bamboo dies off where they live

Page 70
1. trace fossil
2. petrified remain
3. original remains
4. index fossil
5. mold
6. mold
7. trace fossil
8. original remains
9. cast
10. trace fossil

Page 71
1. A. crust; B. mantle; C. outer core; D. inner core
2. inner core
3. outer core
4. crust
5. mantle
6. mantle
7. outer core
8. inner core
9. crust
10. crust

Page 72
1. Two plates slide past one another.
2. An ocean plate is subducting under a continental plate. This causes earthquakes.
3. Plates move away from each other and molten rock fills in the gap.
4. The San Andreas Fault is located at a transform-fault boundary where the Pacific Plate is slipping past the North American Plate
5. Plate interactions can cause stress between the plates, and the rocks can only take so much stress. An earthquake is a result of a release of stress.

Page 73
1. A
2. H
3. C
4. J
5. B
6. F
7. D

Page 74
1. A
2. G
3. C
4. J
5. B
6. F
7. B
8. H
9. C

Page 75
1. igneous rock
2. sediments
3. sedimentary rock
4. metamorphic
5. magma
6. sedimentary
7. igneous
8. metamorphic

9. igneous
10. sedimentary

Page 76
1. Possible answer: Plant C was growing in very sandy soil, and the water drained too quickly from the soil.
2. Possible answer: The store-bought potting soil contains a similar composition and nutrients to the soil used for Plant D.
3. Possible answer: Plant growth is dependent upon soil composition. The best plant growth occurs when there is a mixture of soil that allows the water to drain slowly, provides nutrients for the growing plant, and is blocky enough so that the roots can cling onto the soil.
4. Possible answer: Since they did not keep temperature the same, all their results are now questionable, since temperature may have affected growth.

Page 77
1. C
2. F
3. B
4. H
5. C
6. J
7. D
8. G

Page 78
1. A
2. J
3. C
4. ozone
5. troposphere; temperature decreases
6. Temperature increases because the ozone layer absorbs the sun's ultraviolet energy.
7. decreases
8. Possible answer: The greenhouse effect is the term used to describe what happens when atmospheric gases such as carbon dioxide and water vapor prevent radiation from leaving Earth's surface. It can be harmful if too much energy remains at the surface.

Page 79
1. B
2. G
3. C
4. H
5. D
6. F
7. A

Page 80
1. B
2. F
3. A
4. G
5. D
6. J
7. D
8. G

Page 81
1. Sun
2. Mercury
3. Venus
4. Earth
5. Mars
6. asteroid belt
7. Jupiter
8. Saturn
9. Uranus
10. Neptune
11. Pluto

Page 82
1. The orbital plane of the planetary objects is relatively flat, with a few planetary orbits tilted slightly from the plane. The shape of the orbits is elliptical (oval) with the sun at one focus of the ellipse.
2. Mercury, Venus, Earth, Mars. Mercury has no atmosphere. Because it is so close to the sun, the sunlit side is very hot and the night side is cold. Venus has a thick atmosphere largely composed of carbon dioxide, which traps solar radiation. This greenhouse effect, and the nearness of the sun, keep Venus very hot. Earth has an atmosphere largely composed of nitrogen and oxygen. Trace amounts of carbon dioxide trap enough heat to keep it pleasant. Mars has an atmosphere that is much thinner than that of Venus or Earth, largely composed of carbon dioxide. It is too thin to trap much heat. This and the greater distance of the sun keep Mars cold.
3. Sunspots are dark spots on the photosphere of the sun, and are cooler than the photosphere, except for the area in the immediate vicinity. These areas are hotter than the photosphere.
4. Solar flares are solar wind bursts that tend to rise up in areas of high sunspot activity. As the solar wind blows towards Earth, electrically charged particles are trapped in Earth's atmosphere and create auroras by ionizing gases in the upper atmosphere.
5. The further a planetary object is from the sun, the slower it moves in its revolution because the gravitational attraction between the planetary objects and the sun decreases with distance from the sun.

Page 83
1. dwarf planet, planet, star, solar system, galaxy
2. constellation
3. Ursa Minor (Little Dipper is also acceptable)
4. fusion
5. supernova
6. spiral, elliptical, and irregular
7. black hole
8. temperature
9. nebula
10. light year
11. spiral

12. As Earth orbits the sun, some constellations come into view while others disappear. Also, some constellations are viewable all year because of their unique positions.

Page 84
1. one day; one year
2. The earth turns counterclockwise on its axis once in 24 hours, and during that time, the sun stays in one place. It is this counterclockwise rotation of Earth that makes the sun appear to rise in the east and set in the west.
3. counterclockwise
4. In the Southern Hemisphere the seasons would be the reverse of what the seasons are in the Northern Hemisphere.
5. D
6. G
7. A
8. H

Page 85
1. the force of gravity acting on the object
2. Planet X, because it has more mass. The weight of an object depends on a planet's mass.
3. Planet Q, because the person's weight, or the force of gravity acting on the person, would be less.
4. The force of gravity, or weight of an object, on a planet depends on the planet's mass and radius. The radius of a planet is the distance from the surface to the center of a planet. Since Planet X and Planet Y have different radii, the forces of gravity acting on the planets are different.

Page 86
1. D
2. G
3. C
4. F
5. C
6. H
7. D

Page 87
8. F
9. B
10. H

Page 88
11. A
12. H
13. A
14. G
15. D
16. F
17. B

Page 89
18. J
19. C
20. H
21. B
22. H
23. A

24. H
25. D

Page 90
26. F
27. B
28. F
29. C
30. F
31. D
32. H

Page 91
33. C
34. J
35. D
36. H
37. A
38. H